BE GOOD SWEET MAID

Golden Memories of Navy Blue

By

MARGARET BOLAND ELLIS

Magnolia Mansions Press

Magnolia Mansions Press
Mobile, Alabama

Be Good Sweet Maid
Golden Memories of Navy Blue

First Printing, April 1983
Second Printing, July, 2005

ISBN 0-9665175-0-4

Art cover and design by Carolyn Miller Design
Photo by Margaret Boland Ellis

Magnolia Mansions Press

Magnolia Mansions Press
4661 Pinewood Drive East
Mobile, Alabama 36618
Email: magnoliamansions@aol.com

This book is dedicated to all those people who made being at the 'W' in the mid-forties so special, but most of all it is to Jean and Betty, who came into my life then and stayed forever.

Be good sweet maid, and let who will be clever;
Do noble things, not dream them, all day long.
And so make Life, Death, and that vast Forever
One grand sweet song.

Charles Kingsley—A Farewell
(1819-1875)

CHAPTERS

CHAPTER 1

GOLDEN MEMORIES OF NAVY BLUE

I HAVE BEEN WRITING THIS BOOK ABOUT Mississippi State College for Women (now Mississippi University for Women) for the past 30 years. It is only recently that I put it on paper. Even as they were happening, I knew that these stories made marvelous memories. Fortunately I jotted down some notes. But, like good wine, they had to age.

When Marcie Sanders (then Alumnae Secretary) wrote asking for contributions to the 100th Anniversary celebration, I got out those notes and began to write some of these experiences. Then the floodgates opened. The bits and pieces I had been filing in the computer of my mind and in the back recesses of my desk drawers all those years came tumbling out.

Though I have used some poetic license in the interest of better journalism, most of the recollections happened exactly as they are retold. Some of the people mentioned I have seen through the years; others I have lost all track of. You may recognize yourself or others. If you wish, you may put yourself in any role for similar things happened to many people.

I have gone back to Columbus often since my student days—taking prospective students, visiting my daughter when she was enrolled, or attending alumnae board meetings or homecomings. The last time I visited the 'W' , I went back to a dorm room where I had once lived. Do the walls recognize me as I do them? Deep within their plaster do small vibrations of old conversations remain? Pray not. But where are all the dreams and all the hopes we had?

Whenever I walk across the campus now, I am overwhelmed with a feeling that says "I love this place." How ironic this is because when so many of us attended, we said we hated it. It was the "in thing" to complain and gripe about everything then. I believe this is still a custom on college campuses today. But even then, perhaps we sensed that the 'W' was giving us some of the best times of our lives. And it did. Maybe this is why the only recurring dream I ever have is the one where I am again a student at MSCW.

As I write this in July of 1982, the Supreme Court has just ruled that MUW must admit males to its nursing school. What this will do to the 'W' as we know it, no one knows. It may make many of us realize we never knew who much we loved the place until we lost it. Years of college are glorious years—freedom from parental control, yet not entirely independent. These are the years when lifetime standards of values are established. These are the times when we make lifetime friends. Truly college days are, as the song from *The Student Prince* tells us, "golden days of our youth."

Returning to the 'W' campus either in person or in memory brings mixed emotions. I shall not pass this way again—yet here I am.

"*Golden days of our youth, golden days.*"

GOLDEN MEMORIES OF NAVY BLUE.

CHAPTER 2

ALONG THE SHORES OF THE BEAUTIFUL TOMBIGBEE

"NEVER WILL I EVER GO TO MSCW," I said not once but over and over during my last couple of years at Meridian High School. Sometimes I said I would go to Ole Miss. The next week I was going to the University of Alabama, which was closer in miles to my home town than the University of Mississippi. People over at Alabama were writing lots of first novels and I wanted to be a writer. The brother of one of my high school basketball teammates had just published one. Professor Hudson Strode was to encourage and inspire many more young writers in Tuscaloosa, but I was not destined to be one of them.

My mother thought it would be a splendid idea for me to go to the 'W', which is probably why I stated so emphatically that I would not go. Teenagers have that way about them. Knowing this does not help, especially now that I have my own teenagers, but that's the way it has always been.

So it was not my mother who talked me into heading to Columbus. No one talked me into it. I was invited to visit the campus during my senior year by some Episcopalians I had met at Camp Bratton-Green. That was the diocese of Mississippi's summer youth camp, and those of us who attended it through our high school years formed some strong bonds of friendship. We did a lot of visiting all over Mississippi.

Whether it was the charm of the campus or the enthusiasm of the Episcopalians, I returned to Meridian and announced to the amazement of my mother, my friends, and my high school teachers, in that order, that I had decided to enroll at MSCW. One visit, one weekend. The 'W' is that kind of place. To the further surprise of everyone, having once committed myself to heart north to Columbus, I never again wavered over where I should attend college.

And thus I departed on September 21, 1943 for MSCW's forty-two acre campus (at that time) in the city of Columbus, "along the shores of the beautiful Tombigbee." That's what the catalog further stated. Semesters started much later in the fall in those times. That is not all that was different. Among many other things, there were no "alphabet soup" requirements such as ACT and SAT. A student could show up on registration day with proper high school credentials and be admitted.

We were in the middle of World War II. No family in the country had been spared being caught up in the drama of a world turned upside down. Almost all of the boys in my high school class had long since gone to the service, many of them having been graduated early. Everything was rationed—shoes, coffee, butter, meat, gasoline. New cars had not been manufactured since 1941, and it was impossible to get tires for those on the roads. No one flew the airlines without high priority, but we did have trains. More about them later.

My journey to my first college day was in the car of a friend with several other freshmen students. Driven by the friend's mother, the car was very crowded even though all trunks and much luggage had been shipped ahead early by Railway Express.

After my momentous decision to go to the 'W', my mother and I had spent a frantic summer gathering navy blue clothing. The uniform was very much a part of MSCW in 1943. The catalog stated the uniform made for a democracy, and being a democracy was very important with Hitler running rampart over Europe. It was difficult to find navy skirts or dresses, and next to impossible to secure navy blue shirts or blouses. We heard the U.S.Navy had bought up all the navy blue dye. Probably that was an exaggeration, but it added to the fever of the search. Another summer rumor spread through town that freshmen had to have navy blue sheets, pillow cases, towels and pajamas, but I knew better. After all, I had been there for one weekend visit, remember?

Those friends who had decided to go to Ole Miss and Alabama

told tales of how any young man attempting to visit a young woman behind the famous iron fence on the front campus of Mississippi State College for Women would get only a running glimpse at the moon and the night watchman. (Security was a term to be developed much later.)

That didn't bother me. Most of the guys I knew were far away in the service. Surely there was more to do in college than just date. That going to class and getting an education was one of them did not occur to my thinking strongly at the time. There were a few fellows about, usually somebody's little brother or classified 4F. There weren't that many civilian men in any college anywhere so I did not consider dating at MSCW a problem any more than at any other place.

People said being a hot shot in your own high school didn't mean a thing when you got to college. They also reported that people got homesick and cried for weeks without stopping.

I felt very confident about departing for college but I can't say I didn't ponder these things in my heart as the car wound its way up U.S Highway 45 at the top wartime speed of 35 mph. Lauderdale went by, Porterville, nearly deserted Electric Mills, Scooba, Shuqualak (pronounced "Sugar Lock"). Later we could always win bets on how to spell Shuqualak when we rode down that highway, especially with people from the Delta who did not know a world existed outside that oval of rich flatland that is said to begin in the lobby of the Peabody Hotel in Memphis and extend southward to its termination in Vicksburg.

Northward after Macon on Highway 45, there is only the fork in the road at Brooksville, right goes to the 'W', and left to Mississippi State University.

The closer we got, the quieter the occupants of the car became. Only my friend's mother continued to chatter. The rest of us were thinking the things freshmen think. The idea of leaving home sounds so good until the moment comes to go.

U.S. 45 approaches Columbus from the "flats", but because the city is set on a hill, the tower of the Methodist Church can be seen from some distance out. The road runs past the usual gas stations, a ratty looking motel that has been there forever, and suddenly there is that narrow steel bridge crossing the Tombigbee River. The river wasn't and isn't very beautiful. It is nearly always muddy with the currents swirling around the pilings of the old cement supports. The cage-like bridge with its overhead girders is no narrow that passing a car in the middle of it is to this very day an experience to set one's nerves on edge.

Once across the structure, the road climbs quickly into the main street of Columbus. The morning of our freshman arrival, the sun was shining brightly. Suddenly I felt a tremendous excitement. I looked back once more at the Tombigbee bridge and the road toward Meridian. The old saying is: "Once you go off to college, you never come home again." We could now see the 'W' clock tower, marking as it has through the years, the campus of MSCW. I wondered what the future held in store for me.

CHAPTER THREE

VENI, VIDI—FINIS

IF THERE IS ANYTHING SYNONYMOUS WITH THE gathering of 'W' girls, it is the squealing and screaming of greetings that occur whenever two or more of them meet. Times come and go, clothing fads wax and wane, social customs change, but that 'W' greeting goes on forever. We got out of the car to a chorus of that noise.

A group of navy blue clad creatures descended upon us with hellos and welcomes, smiles and offers to help.

"We are your 'Y' sponsors," they screamed.

"Why?" we asked.

"Not 'why', 'Y' as in YWCA. We are your hostesses. We want to make you feel at home."

I thought that if I had wanted to feel at home, I would have stayed there, but having been "brought up" to be polite, I smiled and said, "That's nice."

The welcoming committee swarmed around the car, asking for things to carry in. They patted us on the back and told us how glad they were that we had come to the 'W'. Any directions they were attempting to give us were lost in the confusion of everyone talking at once.

First things first. Orientation week was first. Freshmen were permitted to wear regular clothes for this period of adjustment. Later we would put on the uniforms of navy blue. This method of dressing labeled newcomers far more effectively than any freshman cap of name tag could have ever done.

The first few days we had a lot of meetings and they all began very early in the morning. The rest of the year, and indeed, my entire time at MSCW would begin early in the morning. Who among those who have attended that institution can ever forget the steam whistle blowing at "twenty till" seven a.m.?

We had meetings to have the rules and regulations of the college explained to us. We had meetings to decide what courses to take. We had meetings to meet people. And, we had meetings to learn the words to all the songs ever written about or sung at Industrial Institute and College and MSCW. And we HAD to learn the words to all the verses of the 'W' songs by the end of the week. This included the Alma Mater ('*In our heart of hearts*,' the other one wasn't to be written until years later). *Hail to Thee, Oh Towered Clock, Magnolia Chain*. Not to know them was to bring a fate worse than death, we were told by upperclassmen. They could stop us at any time or place on campus and demand that we recite whatever verse to whatever song they named. So learn the words we did.

Maybe it was wrong to force this issue. Now I think not because I can still sing nearly every one of them. I find it sad, even shocking, to attend Homecoming ceremonies or graduation and find the modern students don't appear to know even the first verse of anything, let alone enough words to sing a song all the way through.

But let me go back to that morning of the checking-in freshman year. I had been assigned to Calloway Hall, always a favorite dorm of freshmen. I stood in line and tried to think up things to say to my 'Y' sponsor who was still hovering over me. It seemed to take a very long time, but finally I got up to a desk where a woman sat surrounded by a stack of papers.

"Where is your slip?" she asked.

I blushed. Was I suffering the horrible fate every Southern girl had been taught to dread—being "seen through?"

"It's under my clothes." I stammered, trying not to look down.

"No, no," she said. "I mean your room slip that we sent you this summer."

"It's in my jewelry box, inside my stationery box, inside my trunk that got sent Railway Express," I said and smiled weakly.

"I'll get the duplicate," she said patiently.

I was to be in room 62 on the third floor.

"Come on. I'll show you where it is,' said my ever helpful 'Y' girl.

I knew where it was. I had stayed in Calloway during my weekend visit. I wanted to show off my knowledge to the other freshmen, but this too-helpful person was interfering. There seemed to be no way to get rid of her, so I gathered the things I had in the car and followed her up the 72 steps to the third floor of Calloway.

If you don't believe there are 72 of them, you may go and count them yourself. Over the next nine months, I memorized them going up and down what seemed to be at least a million times. There was an elevator, but it was operated manually, requiring that a large rope be pulled hand-over-hand to slowly raise the cage. It was off limits to all but maintenance personnel moving trunks.

At the end of the 72 steps we walked down the hall and around the corner. Room 62 was the first room on the right. My two roommates had not yet arrived, but the room was crowded with three trunks which had been delivered by Railway Express. One of my two roommates was a girl I had known at Camp Bratton-Green, "Tootsie" Spivey. The other I had not met, but she had a good old Southern double name, Iva Jane Patterson

Later we affectionately called her nothing but "Pitty Pat." Since neither of them had arrived, the 'Y' sponsor sat down on the bare mattress of one of the beds as if to stay awhile. I was really feeling a bit annoyed by her presence. I had been on campus several hours, taken care of some necessary items on my own, and I felt quite capable of carrying on without her help. I wanted to get into my trunk and start some unpacking.

She got up and said, "I'll come by and get you to go to supper, only they call it dinner up here. It is at six o'clock in Shattuck."

I knew that. I had eaten there. I was a freshman now and I could handle anything.

"By the way," she said as she turned to leave, "don't let any of the upperclassmen fool you into buying a chapel seat, a subscription to the college newspaper, or a yearbook. They are all included in your matriculation fee. You'll pay that when you register for classes. Some of the older students like to fool you freshmen."

I said goodbye and closed the door. Maybe there was a place in my life for the 'Y' sponsor after all. I reached into my pocket. With a deep sign, I pulled out the receipts for a chapel seat, the college newspaper and the yearbook and tore them into tiny little pieces.

CHAPTER FOUR

THE HOUR OF THE TOWER

THE CLOCK TOWER OF CALLOWAY HALL is one of the oldest buildings on the campus, and also one of the most famous. If any one image calls up the vision of the MSCW campus, it is the clock tower. It has been printed and engraved and featured on catalog and yearbook covers nearly the whole hundred years of the school's existence.

The clock in the tower has been recording the passing of time all those hours. It ran faithfully during the war years when we were freshmen and sophomores and chimed the hour and the half-hour during the day and night, constantly reminding all who heard that time and life were hurrying by. The solo ring was and still is a lonesome sound in the dead of the night. It could create panic as it began to strike 10 p.m. in those attempting to make the dorm doors before they were locked. It is amazing how fast students could move before the ten strokes were completed.

Those people who lived in the rooms near the bell chamber were less enthusiastic about the usefulness of the ringing especially during test or exam times. It told more of the passing hours than we cared to know. I was one of those people weary of living under the clock tower.

Calloway had served so long as a student dormitory that it had gone through at least one remodeling prior to my arrival in 1943. But then, as now, the fourth floor remained as it had during the early 1900s. Doors protecting the stairs to that top floor were locked at all times. It was forbidden to go to the fourth floor. It was "not safe," we were told. How it was safe to live on the third floor under the "unsafe" fourth floor was never explained.

That rule itself was enough to make enterprising freshmen through the years quickly find ways to unlock the doors. In our case, we found by trial and error a key that locked a room closet would also unlock one of the fourth floor stairway doors.

Once on the forbidden floor, we found antiquated rooms and hallways. The whole area was dim and dusty and hung with cobwebs of many years. Pieces of broken furniture were scattered about. Part of a bed, a three legged chair, and an old desk were thrown into a corner. The windows were streaked with grime, filtering the light that entered into a gray haze. Footprints made patterns in the dust on the floor.

Entrance to the clock tower was available from this floor. The inside of the chamber was not painted, but made of big unfinished timbers. There were steep narrow steps which curled upward. Students of former days had dared to leave their names written in chalk and paint on the rough-hewed boards from which the inside of the tower was constructed.

We made many trips to the fourth floor and the tower. A literature buff thought of the line, "*Childe Roland to the dark tower came,*" and we chanted it as we mounted the steps. There was a rumor back then that if someone was in the tower when the clock struck, that person would fall dead. This seemed to us to defy all physical and logical explanation, so we refused to believe it. The clock was completely mechanical so there was no danger of electricity. We were nevertheless somewhat nervous when the hour neared and we knew the clock would soon start to strike. No one could get up quite enough nerve to stay there when the clock struck to find out for sure.

During freshman mid-term exams we determined to silence the chiming of the clock so that our studying and our sleep would not be disturbed. How to do it occupied much of our thinking and conversations.

After a brainstorming session that probably might better have been spent studying, we decided to collect some cardboard boxes for our project. We took them to the fourth floor of Calloway. There we tore them into large rectangular pieces. We then took them up the steep and winding stairway to the clock mechanism and taped layers of the heavy box sides to the bell of the clock on the spot where the hammer hit. We then rushed breathlessly down the steps, on to the third floor, carefully locking the door behind us.

Soon the hour approached. It was working! When the clock struck there was only a muffled thud. We snickered every time this happened, but were also amazed and a little disappointed that many people did not even realize the clock bell was not ringing normally.

About a week later the clock began to regain its voice, and we climbed up and tore off the remnants of the boxes. The hammer had finally worn a hole where it hit.

Near the end or our freshman year, we decided to climb one last time. We had two objectives this trip. One was to take pictures from the small louvered windows at the very top of the tower over the clock itself. That was then the highest point of the campus and it was a marvelous panoramic view. The second reason for this trip was that we had decided to record our names and the dates along with the many others before us. We reasoned that by the time they were discovered, if ever, we would be far enough gone to escape any punishment.

My name was discovered all right—thirty years later. With pounding heart and ear tuned to housemothers who might come to investigate, a freshman member of the class of 1980 climbed the old clock tower.

There she discovered my name, as she put it, "Written in pink fingernail polish, of all things, Mother!" and she promptly and proudly continued the tradition of the second generation and put her name beneath mine in the old clock tower.

CHAPTER FIVE

IN CASE OF FIRE, JUMP ON IN

WE USED TO GO AROUND IN CIRCLES to get away from it all in Calloway back in the school year of 1943-44. At that time, fire escapes were tall black cylinders which ran up the walls of dorms Calloway, Columbus, and Hastings. They stood like great smokestacks poking their way to the edge of the building roofs. Inside were tight, spiral, steel slides, which circled from the third floor, past the second and on to the ground level. They were not unlike giant conch shells. These strange looking structures no doubt satisfied the fire codes of the day. They also served several other useful purposes for 'W' girls of the era.

There were, as we have been noting, rules for everything in the forties; and there certainly was a rule saying don't use the fire escape unless there is a real fire or a fire drill. Freely translated that meant "Don't play on the fire escapes and certainly don't slide down them unless absolutely necessary."

Fire drills were held periodically. At the ringing of the fire bell, students were supposed to take a laundry bag, sit on it, and make an orderly downward trip through the big cylinder. The laundry bag was to protect clothing, and on some days, backside skin for the slides became very tacky on moist, humid days. On such days, gravity would hardly carry a person down and it was necessary to push forward and backward to get momentum to move at all. On these sticky days, there were frequent logjams of people, too, slowing down the "escape time" which was being checked by officials and administrators during the drills.

Entrance to the fire escape on the second and third floor of Calloway was from the end rooms on each hall. This was a nuisance to those girls who lived in the rooms. Thrill and curiosity seekers were constantly coming in and asking to try out the slide down at times other than legitimate fire drills. Neither was it at all unusual to see someone come zipping out about 6:58 a.m. Once the doors to Shattuck dining hall closed at 7 a.m., there was no getting breakfast. Fast food places hadn't even been thought of in those days, and few students had funds to purchase a doughnut and coffee at the Golden Goose Tearoom.

The girls on our third floor hall who lived in the escape-door room were friends of the people who lived directly below them on second floor. Rather than walk down the hall, down the stairs, and back down the hall, the third floor folks often took a short cut by sliding from third to second. Catching the second floor opening as on slid by was a bit tricky, but it did save a lot of time and walking.

One night a third floor girl decided to take this way down. She slipped into the fire escape, sped down, but missed the second floor door. She slid on and down and zoomed out the fire escape into the courtyard in the midst of several couple of 'W' girls and their dates from State. This dropping-in was particularly significant because at the time the slider was wearing only a slip.

Dorm doors were locked week nights at 10 p.m. in the forties, but a person with agility and athletic skill could sneak in late by climbing UP the fire escape. Admittedly this was not easy, but the penalties of arriving after the dorm doors were shut were to be avoided at any cost.

Crawling up was impossible, but if one's back were put to the center pole, and feet positioned on the outer walls of the steel tube, it was possible to walk the feet up the outside wall and gradually cork-screw higher and higher until the second floor entrance was reached. All this work was in vain if, by appearing in the reverse, as it were, and coming in the fire escape door into that dorm room startled its occupant. Many a student worked thirty minutes on this arduous climb only to frighten the inhabitant of the room into blood-curdling screams. This promptly brought large crowds of people into the halls, also summoning the housemother to investigate the cause of such disruptions. Thus the success of the climb could be nullified if one was not careful. Guess how I found this out?

With modernization, the fire escapes have disappeared. Not one is left standing, not even for historical or sentimental reason. Shrills and shrieks that were heard during the fire drills have been silenced. There is no more slipping in and out by this method. These adventures and their reasons for being have joined the other ghosts of the past.

CHAPTER SIX

THE LITTLE MISSISSIPPI

THE MISSISSIPPI RIVER ONCE FLOWED THROUGH the back part of the 'W' campus. Well, okay, so it wasn't THE Mighty Mississippi, but it was called the "Little Mississippi." It meandered through the rose garden behind the former Home Economics practice houses, and it did resemble a scale model of the great water that marks the western border of our Magnolia state.

The little stream made a pretty sight as it flowed through the flowers and it was a stop on all the visitors' tours given by Mrs. Burney L. Parkinson, wife of the president. My memory of it is not of the beauty it afforded but of another entirely different kind of stop.

But let me start at the beginning—of the story, not the river. In 1943 study hall hours were strictly enforced. From 7 p.m. to 9:30 p.m. freshmen had to be either in their own rooms studying, or whatever posed as studying, or at the library. Going to the library was more fun, and more productive.

Once the 9:30 p.m. bell rang, freshmen had thirty minutes until dorm closing time to go to The Goose for food and drinks. Coming and going to the library was not monitored. Freshmen often left early. We would stand around in the shadows near The Goose, which was then located where the green and gazebo now are located, waiting for the signal to end the study hall and admit us to the social pleasures of the refreshment place.

The bell which proclaimed the end of this restriction and the beginning of the freedom was on a pole on the driveway side of Shattuck Hall. It was about the size of a railway locomotive bell and was sounded by pulling a rope which hung from it.

Naturally we freshmen thought of the daring idea to ring the bell early. We came up with a plan that would enable us to commit this "crime" and get safely away. Two or three of us would bicycle from the back side of Shattuck to the bell pole. A few good tugs would sound the bell. Then we would jump on bikes and ride quickly around the old tennis courts and behind Peyton Hall, by the old laundry and come out in the area by Reneau and the Home Ec houses.

From there we would proceed slowly and nonchalantly to The Goose as if we knew nothing except that it was time for study hall to be over and our social half hour to begin.

The plan worked beautifully. We enjoyed the extended snack periods, but even more we relished the fact that we were getting by with this deception. And so we did for awhile. We did not ring the bell early every night lest we spoil a good thing. It was the sophomores, only one step higher on the college ladder than freshmen but determined that we should pay our dues, who put a stop to our early admissions to The Goose. When they figured out what was happening, they knew it had to be done by freshmen. Who else would care when the bell rang? Upperclassmen were not governed by it. Besides it was the job of the sophomore who worked in the Shattuck Hall office on the evening shift to ring the bell and she, although having never enjoyed the job, did not like someone else doing it for her. She had been called down for ringing it early and that had not set well with her at all. She tipped off some of her sophomore buddies and one evening they determined to catch us.

They stationed themselves in strategic positions along our chosen path. This was, of course, completely unknown and unsuspected by us. As usual two of us freshmen slipped around the back way and rang the bell fifteen minutes early. We had grown daring as time went by. We hopped on our bakes and sped through the back way as we had done in the past. As we rounded the curve behind the infirmary, the sophomores jumped out of the dark behind the bushes, waved their arms and shouted.

"Stop. You there, stop!"

We did not recognize the sophomores or their voices and thought we had been caught by administrative personnel. We bike riders split in two directions. Where my partner in crime went that night I never knew. I took the path behind the Home Ec houses toward the rose garden.

It was totally black in the area and I was riding hard. Unable to see where I was going, but determined to get away; I pedaled straight into the "Little Mississippi." Like its counterpart, it just kept rolling along... I did not. The front wheel of the bicycle pitched into a deep spot in the water sending me over the handlebars and into another bend of this scenic waterway.

I sat there while the water seeped slowly through my clothes. At any moment I expected my pursuers to come crashing through the rose garden and find me, but no one ever did. I didn't even go to The Goose that night.

CHAPTER SEVEN

NOT QUITE NINETY-NINE BOTTLES OF BEER ON THE WALL

WHEN ARCHAEOLOGISTS DIG INTO OUR CIVILIZATION centuries from now, I am convinced they will divide our era into three cultures—the long-neck beer bottle, the steel beer can, and the aluminum beer can.

This particular story will deal with the long-neck bottle era, for indeed in the World War II years, nothing else had been developed. There was not that much beer available to anyone. That Mississippi had been a dry state since the end of prohibition is another story in itself. The state had its bootleggers who delivered "white lightning" in fruit jars. Here, too, were the beginnings of the black market bonded era which would in time lead to the infamous "black market tax."

But college students wanted beer; and beer was scarce during the forties. The only brand that ever seemed to be available was called Lion. We didn't have television and consequently no television commercials telling us to head for the mountains, or that if we had the time, they had the beer. Nobody said, "This one's for you." Getting beer for anybody took some knowing the right people, and the right place, and the right price. The Lion brand had a label with a picture of the king of beasts standing there looking very fierce. That was a clue to the taste coming. The lion's tail curled about his hind legs with a bushy tassel at the end. Taste buds curled about one's eyeteeth with one sip of the Lion's brew. I don't think I can ever forget how bad it was, simply dreadful, I feel sure by any standards. Beer is said to be an acquired taste; and at that stage in my life, I definitely had not acquired that taste. Having the experience of drinking Lion first, it is a wonder that any of us ever tried anything else. However, then as now, college students thought it was necessary to drink beer in order to be college students.

The rules of the Parkinson era were strict and enforced to the letter of the law. There were regulations covering every conceivable situation. An entire chapter of this volume will be given over to describing them in detail. It goes without saying that drinking was the most cardinal of sins, the worst thing a young lady at the 'W' could ever do—well almost the worst—the very worst could not even be discussed it was so unthinkable. It was said that the mere whiff of a mouthwash high in alcoholic content was serious enough to cause a student to be campused. A tablespoon of beer could mean certain expulsion. And the law was swift in those days. Such extended litigation as civil rights and appeals did not exist in courts then. So the very smell of alcohol spelled doomsday.

But, just as in the days of prohibition and thereafter, laws against alcohol and drinking cannot be legislated. Ever since the first caveman found that his grapes left too long in the basket produced an exotic liquid, many of the human species have chosen to indulge.

With the production of alcohol for civilian consumption greatly lessened by the war effort, spirits were hard to come by in the best of circumstances. In the worst of circumstances being a 'W' student and securing any fruit of the vine or the hops required the expertise of an international spy and a network of suppliers one notch below the Manhattan Project. Did this stop the 'W' student body from procuring alcohol? Not by a Tiffany wine glass it didn't!

In later years colorful places like "The Pad" would grow up, and legends about them would become a part of the 'W' culture and tradition. Somehow the 'W' underground has always known where the stuff was and dared to get it. Consider how few students had cars during the war, and the magnitude of that operation increases.

It should be pointed out at this time that long-neck bottles were heavy, that they required a bottle opener, they were at that time returnable, but they were NOT readily nor easily disposed of.

Consider too, that they could in no way be put into waste baskets in dorm rooms, hall trash containers, or even outside garbage cans anywhere on campus. The risk of being tracked down was ever present. If you think smuggling beer into the dorms was hard work, it was nothing compared to getting the empty bottles out.

Bringing them in was a challenge and a status symbol, removing them—empty—was a chance no one wanted to take. So they were hidden in closets as they accumulated, not just tossed in with the shoes and the laundry bag, but very carefully tucked away. There were, after all, room inspections each week. The checking for "bunny tails" (balls of dust) was thorough. Anything as odd-shaped as a long-neck beer bottle was sure to be seen and pulled out.

The obvious place to store the bottle was in suitcases. At least travel bags would not be opened during inspection. They were usually pushed to the back of the closet or more often stored in closets down the hall. Travel was very limited and the 'W' was not "Suitcase University" that it became in later times. Luggage was rarely used except during holiday periods or perhaps one or two weekends each semester.

Once when our source of beer had temporarily dried up, we decided to make our own. As someone remarked, we had the bottles! So while living in Reneau as a sophomore, we determined to try our own hand at bathtub brew, only of course, we could not use the bathtub.

A girl who lived on our wing claimed to know how to make beer. Nobody challenged her recipe. We bicycled to a nearby grocery store and purchased a can of liquid malt. That product was carried for years in the section of the store where syrup was kept. It is possible to find it still in some places. Sugar was rationed, but we hoarded bits and bags, accumulated from the dining hall over a period of many weeks. We also bought several cakes of yeast—it didn't come powdered then. Several of us pooled our remaining resources and purchased an earthenware churn from a local hardware store. In it we mixed all the ingredients, carefully adding several quarts of water. Next the jar had to be transported to the top floor of Reneau, the fifth floor. Getting to the fourth floor was not the problem. There were stairs to that level where there were four rooms inhabited by students and a very large sleeping porch which ran the length of one side of the hall. Getting the churn to the fifth floor was the hard part. There was a choice of going straight up a vertical ladder and through a trap door, or taking the elevator.

Reneau, just as Calloway, had an elevator, operated by hand rope, but it was not possible to operate the mechanism without creating a great deal of noise. The pulleys creaked and squeaked, and the big rope bumped the sides of the shaft. In order to move the unappetizing and smelly liquid, we decided to skip lunch one day. With the dorm vacated by most students, but especially by the social adviser, we got the elevator going and cranked it up to the fifth floor, where we unloaded the vat. There we hid it behind some dusty trunks which had been in storage since September.

It did not take long at all for a very powerful aroma to drift down to the upper halls. Within a few days, the definite odor of beer could be smelled on the third floor. Why no one ever checked the top floor remains a mystery. Perhaps they did and either did not discover the churn, or decided to leave it alone. There was little doubt of what was "brewing" for that whole end of the building reeked of beer by the time a few more days had passed. There were all kinds of comments from students. Those not in on the making of the batch, speculated someone had broken a bottle of beer somewhere, and there was going to be hell to pay when the social adviser found out who it was.

We were somewhat concerned that the crock would be found, but then, who could prove who had made the mixture? One of the "brewers" on our wing had some bananas in her window. They had become quite overripe and they, too, were smelling very strongly. We persuaded her to let the bananas keep rotting to cover the smell of the beer. It worked up to a point—the point where the two sets of smells converged—about the third floor stairwell.

Finally we decided that the moment had come to bottle the brew. We unloaded some of the Lion bottles from the suitcases. Someone said they needed to be sterilized, but we could not find anyone willing to wash them thoroughly for fear of being caught while doing that job. A couple of us finally got in the shower with the bottles and washed them with hot soapy water. We planned to do the actual bottling in the storage area on the fifth floor, with one person standing watch while the others did the pouring. We climbed the ladder from fourth floor so we would not have to use the elevator, and there we managed to siphon the liquid from the churn into the bottles—using a section of rubber tubing "borrowed" from the chemistry lab.

Of course we had no way to put on airtight caps, so we wrapped the tops of the bottles with the silver paper that used to come on Hershey chocolate bars. It was not airtight, but that seemed to make little difference. Any life left in the yeast did not blow the foil as might have been anticipated. We let the liquid "age" in the bottles all of two or three days, still hidden in the chambers of the upper floor. The next move was to get the bottles down the ladder and hidden away in someone's room. We finally put them in a waste basket and lowered it with a rope. The earthenware churn was left on the fifth floor. For all I know it may be there still.

Saturday night was party time, so we got our usual waste basket full of ice for ten cents at the old ice house across the street from Reneau. We hid it in a closet with the iced down bottles of home brew.

Why is it that when something like that is going on, everyone senses that something is up but the ones not in the know can't put a finger on it, and the ones who are in on the secret delight in being mysterious? We hinted and bragged and did everything but put out a bulletin on the radio that there was going to be a really big event somewhere on campus Saturday night.

If the Lion brand of beer was horrible, it was nothing but premium compared to our home-brew. Ours was "Old Tennis

Shoe" after a game in the mud without socks; but we all pretended it was the nectar of the gods.

Those bottles were emptied in short order, with some, including part of mine, poured down the sink when no one was looking. We didn't get caught; but we did give up the manufacture of beer for the duration of our college days.

We did not, however, discontinue the consumption of the Lion product when it could be obtained, so the long-necked bottles continued to accumulate in the suitcases. Looking back it really wasn't that much fun, and certainly not worth the risks involved. After a few sips of beer, one did not dare leave the room for fear of the dreaded "breath-test," so partaking was a form of self-imposed imprisonment. But it was a challenge to be met and we met it.

There came that time, however, when we absolutely had to get rid of the beer bottles. No one wanted to take a sack of empty beer bottles from the dorm because there was no place to take it once outside the building. Students had no cars. It seemed a bit much to try to haul a sack away on a bicycle. Columbus citizens were as aware of the MSCW rules as students, and while I never knew of any of them turning in students for violations, it was rumored that they would. Everyone in town could recognize a 'W' girl instantly because of the uniforms we wore. The local folk could hardly be expected to ignore a student on a bicycle depositing a sack of empty beer bottles in a neighborhood garbage can.

As Christmas holidays drew near, we knew there was only one solution. Departing for the vacation, many students had very heavy suitcase which they would allow no one else to touch or carry. Not many clothes went home for the holidays, but the beer bottles were taken out in the Christmas luggage to be disposed of somewhere between the Old Maid's Gate and Hometown, Mississippi.

And on the way home the song was not, "*Ninety-nine bottles of beer on the wall;*" but a hearty rendition of a variation which began "*Ninety-nine bottles without any beer, Ninety-nine bottles are gone.*"

CHAPTER EIGHT

SERENADE IN BLUE

"When I hear that serenade in blue,
I'm somewhere in another world alone with you,
Sharing all the joys we used to know,
Many moons ago."

IN THE SCHOOL YEAR OF 1943-44, the "BLUE SERENADERS" became a campus organization. These were the years of the big band sound, the Glenn Miller arrangements, the time of SWING! It was inevitable that those girls who had come to the 'W' with the ability and training to play musical instruments would sooner or later get together for a "jam" session. If they were going to play, why not an organized group? Why not capitalize on the wearing of the blue uniform and the fact that one of the most popular songs of the day was called *"Serenade in Blue?"* Adopting that melody as their theme song, the orchestra became organized under the first director-leader, Louise "Babe" Stephenson. These girls provided a band sound of current day hits that was not like any other group on campus. They gave students the music and the mood for the Saturday night dances, the "Little Sister" party; and they played in chapel and on many other occasions. They were probably the biggest morale booster during the era, for the sound of music, then as now, was essential to the feelings and welfare of those in school and working during that all-out war effort.

The original Blue Serenaders were Betty Barnes and Vanessa Smith on first saxophone, Martha Harrell, Nell White, and Meriwether Gabbert on second sax; and "Pitty Pat" Patterson on clarinet. Jean Lancaster played first trumpet and Rosie Hahn, second; "Siddy" Spicer, drums; Doris Fleming, trombone; Rose Raney, base fiddle; and Mildred Gillis, piano. Gillis was also willing and very able to play the piano at the conclusion of the noon and especially the evening meals in Shattuck. Many a good time was passed singing or "jitterbugging" to the lively renditions in the front halls outside the dining hall until time for class or study hall to begin. Vocalist for the Serenaders was Ev Lambeth with a lovely, clear, sweet voice. Little did we know how short her song on this earth would be. Ev and Betty Barnes both died not many years after our time at the 'W'.

The first Blue Serenaders wore navy blazers with white skirts. They had band stand boxes like those used by all the big bands. Ours were painted light blue with navy blue lettering of "Blue Serenaders" across the front.

In the second year of The Blue Serenaders, Jean Lancaster took over as director. The musicians had a larger group and the performing outfits were changed to powder blue sweaters with white skirts and blouses. The light blue color was a part of this campus many years before it became part of the adopted "blue on blue" school colors.

The Serenaders in the school year 1944-45 still had Barnes and Harrell on sax but that section had added Fairae Lyn Carter and Carolyn Bateman. Fleming had Bobbie Ruth Aycock to help in the trombone blowing. There were two new clarinet players—Ann Dabney and Jean Ritour. Rosie was still thumping the bass and Gillis the ivories. Lancaster and Hahn remained on trumpet with the help of Sara Bartlett and Rosalind Dottery. The addition of two violins, played by Marjorie Trusty and Eloise Quackenboss, gave the group a really full sound. On drums that year was Sally Slaten. Ev still had the solo vocals. Nell Breyer, Betty Adams, and Mary Alice Wilkins formed a trio that gave the Blue Serenaders even more versatility and a wide range of popular appeal. The 'W' girls in blue did serenade and perform all the top songs of the forties. Do you remember? How could you forget *"A String of Pearls," "Tuxedo Junction," "In the Mood," "Blues in the Night," "Yes, Indeed," "I'll Be Seeing You," "Boogie Woogie"* and the haunting and lovely

"I'll Never Smile Again?"

Remember the pop singers? Bing Crosby, Helen Forrest, Frank Sinatra, (with Tommy Dorsey's orchestra), Vaughn Monroe, Bob Eberly. Would you believe one of the first records on the juke box when it was finally put in The Goose was Doris Day singing *"Sentimental Journey"* with Les Brown and his band of renown? How about the groups? The Ink Spots, The Andrews Sisters, The Pied Pipers, The Three Suns. And those enduring vocalists such as Dinah Shore, Ella Fitzgerald, and Perry Como, troopers who can still belt them out. But ever and always, it was the Glenn Miller era. Who among you out there can ever hear *"Moonlight Serenade," "Pennsylvania 6500," "Chattanooga Choo Choo," "Kalamazoo,"* or *"Stardust"* without an overwhelming wave of nostalgia?

When we couldn't listen to the Blue Serenaders, we got our music from records—heavy, easily-broken 78 rpm records. They only cost 35 and 50 cents, and the record shops would let customers take them into booths and listen for hours without purchasing anything at all. There were more big bands than could be counted and lots of big band radio from Frank Dailey's Meadowbrook Ballroom, a must on everyone's schedule. And record sales began to near the millions.

There were war songs, too. Can you still sing *"Coming in on a Wing and a Prayer"* or *"Praise the Lord and Pass the Ammunition?"* The novelty tunes came around including that crazy one called *"Open the Door, Richard"* and the still popular Andrews Sisters' *"Rum and Coca Cola."* There was a radio show that came on late at night from Cincinnati on that city's clear channel station. It was called "Moon River" and featured poetry read in between dreamy music, played mostly on the organ. Tuning it in meant playing the radio after lights out, but of course, that did not stop anyone from listening to the show.

About the only place the music of the forties can be heard now is on albums reissued by companies who have doctored the original sounds to stereo. If you are lucky sometimes you can catch this wonderful sound "live" at some of the annual reunions of the Auburn Knights or when some of the band members from Mississippi State or Ole Miss get together.

The Blue Serenaders played on at the 'W' until some time in the fifties; and then one year they just didn't organize. They were great. Could they ever again sound the way we remember them? Probably not, but then that doesn't really matter. They were in the right place at the right time, and their music added a dimension to college life that can never be replaced.

"Once again your face comes back to me
Just like the theme of some forgotten melody,
In the album of my memory,
SERENADE IN BLUE."

CHAPTER NINE

EVERYBODY'S MOST UNFORGETTABLE CHARACTER—MISS POHL, WHO ELSE?

"YOU WON'T REMEMBER ME," said the woman at the MSCW Alumnae luncheon, "I'm the girl who couldn't tell her left foot from her right."

Emma Ody Pohl, straight, slim and alert at eighty years of age, looked at the woman and with a twinkle in her eye, answered.

"My dear, don't you know if you HAD known your left foot from your right, then I would have remembered you."

Regardless of the number of years that have passed, her students will always remember Miss Pohl and her two most repeated remarks:

"Don't you know your left foot from your right foot?"

And: "Throw out that chewing gum!"

Miss Pohl shouted those commands at students for nearly half a century at MSCW where she was dancer supreme, head of the department of physical education and avant-garde in ideas. She had a wide audience, for during that period she taught every single student who attended the college, an estimated 50,000.

It all began in 1908 when Miss Pohl set up a program of physical education for the elementary and high schools in her native city of Greenville, Mississippi.

Physical education was a new and daring concept in 1908. When her Greenville program attracted the attention of state superintendent of education, Henry Whitfield, who saw the wisdom of her foresight, dispatched her to II&C to set up the first college program of physical education for women in the state, and one of the first of its kind in the nation. MSCW became the state's first school to require physical education for all women—modified and restricted for those with physical handicaps, but P.E. for all.

Once she arrived on the campus in Columbus, Miss Pohl became as established as the clock tower and never left again except for brief vacations or visiting summer teaching assignments. For the next 47 years this human dynamo was as much a living part of the campus as the ivied walls. She was one of those rare individuals who become legends in their own time.

Miss Pohl's accomplishments were perhaps best exemplified by the dance and the Zouave. It was hard to tell if her first love was the ballet or the students who performed it. Both occupied top priority in her life.

Each spring and fall Miss Pohl's dancers gave a program for capacity crowds in Whitfield auditorium. *"Les Sylphides"* was an all-time favorite. She choreographed most of the dances herself. She once defined the dance as "that act by which you see the things that you feel."

The Zouave drill satisfied her search for some colorful spectacular which would provide campus-wide participation. She learned the drill from Count de Beauviere, a French military expert, who had copied it from the Zouaves, those colorful French colonial troops noted for their precision exhibitions.

First presented on the II&C campus in 1912, Zouave soon became a regional favorite. For many years the spirited music for the drill was traditionally played by neighboring Mississippi State College's band. Stories are still told of Miss Pohl taking the baton and climbing atop the fountain on the front campus to lead the musicians in the exact tempo she was seeking. From that lofty position she could also spot someone chewing gum on the tenth row and roar for the immediate disposal of it.

When President William Howard Taft visited the campus for one of Miss Pohl's gala festivals including Zouave, he went away with the statement, "Not all the generals are on the battlefield."

The last full Zouave was given in 1955, the year of Miss Pohl's retirement. By special invitation, the Third Army Band played. A huge crowd spilled over the campus to watch the thousand or more young women complete the precision marching, formations, mass calisthenics, and fencing drills, all without one single spoken command. Tension and sentiment were running high.

"I'll remember that day forever," said one of the student captains. "We had rehearsed for months, worked hard, and we were tired and keyed up. We all felt that we'd just blow the whole drill. Miss Pohl called a briefing meeting that morning."

"This day is a trying one for you, I know," she said. "It is for me. When I got up this morning, I said to my clothes, if you're going with me today, hang on."

"Everyone laughed," the captain went on, "we relaxed and the drill went to perfection."

At the conclusion of the final performance, a band member laid down his horn. "I've never seen anything like it in my life," he said. Those were the sentiments of nearly everyone who ever saw Zouave and those who were privileged to perform in it. While complaining and protesting through the weeks of preparation, that rare and diminishing group of students who were part of one of Miss Pohl's Zouave drills, now look back with pride and a sense of accomplishment for having been a part of this amazing tradition. There really has never been anything quite like it.

I had heard of Miss Pohl long before I went to MSCW. Everyone in Mississippi "knew" her. She was loved and respected, but because of her wide-spread reputation, most freshmen, myself included, viewed her with awe, fear, and trembling.

During orientation she was pointed out to us more than once. She was a familiar figure moving across the campus with speed and determination that often caused her to be mistaken for a student. I had never personally been introduced to her when shortly after the semester had begun, I reported to a swimming class with Jean Anderson. We were eager for a challenge which we did not feel we would find in the swimming class. The controversial requirement that called for every student to pass a swimming test before being graduated from MSCW posed no problem to those of us who had been swimming all our lives.

When an upperclassman cautioned us, "Don't go in the pool until the instructor gets here," that was all Jean and I needed to leap into the water.

The sound of our splashing brought Miss Pohl herself stalking out of the dressing room, a development we had not anticipated. Miss Pohl pulled off her horn-rimmed glasses. She wore them years before they became fashionable. She wiped off the steam that had accumulated on them from the high humidity of the pool enclosure. She looked at us for a long moment without saying a word. We climbed sheepishly out of the pool. The rest of the class had backed into the wall as if to divorce themselves from our misdeed.

Looking straight at me she said, "What is you name?"

"Boland," I answered, "Margaret Boland."

Then Miss Pohl said, "Boland, (she always called students by their last name), I like girls who dare to be different, but we have rules around here and they are for good reasons and you must abide by them. Do not enter the water now or later unless you are directed to do so by your teacher." With that she put the glasses back on and left.

One night weeks later, Jean and Betty Eskrigge and I went into the gym during study hall and began hitting a tennis ball back and forth across the floor. There was no net nor were there any court lines so we could not really have a game. We were letting off some excess energy rather than study. Miss Pohl appeared from nowhere before we had hit a dozen rallies.

"You cannot play tennis in here during study hour," she said.

"We can't do anything around here," I muttered half-way under my breath but loud enough for her to hear. "We don't have any freedom."

Off came the horn-rimmed glasses again. She waved them at me with an extended arm.

"Boland, you are the young lady who likes to go swimming

before class begins, aren't you?"

"Yes, ma'am."

"Well, let me tell you there is one thing you'd better learn here and now," she said. "Without discipline, there is no freedom. You remember that always!"

This philosophy was instilled into her students at MSCW. And somehow Emma Ody Pohl was able to wave a magic wand in the transformation of young girls into women, women ready to accept their responsibilities in the world whatever their field or calling. She taught not only the advantages of sound minds and healthy bodies; she taught an appreciation for the beautiful and a sense of values. She taught hope and resourcefulness. And she taught discipline as evidenced in the ballet performances and Zouave, discipline of body, but discipline of mind as well.

During the years that she was associated with the college, she taught mothers, their daughters, and before she finally retired, she had granddaughters of former students. Although students held her in fear and awe, she was loved and respected above all. That she was appreciated by all student bodies is evident in the fact that more annuals were dedicated to her by MSCW students than anyone else in the history of the school.

There was such an air of authority about her that when Miss Pohl walked into a room, talking ceased. The energy that remained with her at 80 years of age vibrated about her. She was a strong believer in walking as the best therapy for body and mind and walked up to five miles daily until three weeks before her death June 23, 1966 at age 85.

She also loved to talk about the MSCW spirit. "This spirit is not a remote or theoretical thing—it is a living, growing ideal and an illuminating force, meaning for each student a realization of needs to be met, a vision of opportunities, and an intelligent and vigorous preparation for the meeting of those needs and the grasping of those opportunities. On the campus, it is only the lips and the feet that change from year to year, the spirit endures."

Miss Pohl was often pressed to make comparisons between students of past and present, but she tactfully avoided such comparisons.

"Things don't change much," she said. "They were wearing beehive hairdos when I came to this place and now they are wearing them again. Times change, fashions come and go, but everything which is fundamentally good will remain."

The beautiful physical education complex on the campus of MUW was a living monument to Miss Pohl. (It was later destroyed by a tornado.) She protested the naming of buildings for her, stating they would probably end up being called "Pohl Hall."

After the two incidents of my freshman year, I knew this was a lady worthy of respect. While I was never one of her dancers, I did work with great pride the 1000-watt floodlights for the dance performances. I was more interested in playing basketball or softball, but Miss Pohl was a friend as well to those students who enjoyed sports, being one of the first educators to recognize the great benefits to women of active participation in athletics. It is a great pity that she was not around to be a part of the evolution of intercollegiate athletics. What a cheerleader she would have been!

"Let me tell you what happened recently," she said to me the last time I saw her. She was retired then, but every full of vim and energy, she had volunteered to assist in the alumnae office. Giving freely of her time to MSCW, she arrived daily at 8 a.m. and put in more than eight hours of work without pay.

"They make you live too long and quit working too soon," was her comment.

She frequently was the speaker at alumnae chapter meetings in Mississippi and in neighboring state chapters.

"I was at this alumnae meeting," she said, "and this girl came up and said to me, 'Miss Pohl, I don't know if you remember me. I'm the one who could never learn her right foot from her left.'"

"Did you ever learn it, honey?" I asked.

"No," she replied sweetly.

"Well, how have you got on?"

"Fine," she answered, "and that really put me in my place." But Miss Pohl couldn't be put in any "place." She was already in her place and that was in the hearts of all the students who had known her through the years.

Among her belongings after her death was found a quotation from Edna St.Vincent Millay's *The Lamp And The Bell*. It was one Miss Pohl was fond of quoting to students.

"I tell you I shall never think of you throughout my life without such tenderness as breaks the heart—and I shall think of you whenever I am most happy, whenever I am most sad, whenever I see a beautiful thing. You are a burning lamp to me—a flame the wind cannot blow out, and I shall hold you high in my hand against whatever darkness."

The familiar walk of Emma Ody Pohl is no longer seen crossing the campus of the 'W', hair and skirt flying behind her. But to the thousands of students who walked with her and to those who walk the campus now, "only the lips and feet have gone, the spirit endures."

CHAPTER TEN

CORKY'S REVENGE

DON'T BELIEVE IT WHEN YOU ARE TOLD there is no such thing as perpetual motion. The bridge game which went on in room 54 in Reneau Hall in the school year 1944-45 never stopped. There were pauses from time to time to go eat, to sleep (never before midnight), and maybe even once in awhile to go to class. but the cards were always in place and they seldom got cold as they were shuffled from one pair of hands to another.

There was a game going on before breakfast, after breakfast, between classes, before lunch—you get the idea. On some occasions, a second game would be started but that seldom lasted. The main attraction was THE game with four players and all the rest of the people who came in and out to kibitz. There was always a standby to slip into a hand and take over should someone leave for whatever reason.

During these bridge sessions, all the problems of the world were contemplated and some even solved. It was during one of these bridge games that we thought up Corky's revenge. But it is necessary to begin as good stories do, at the beginning.

Babe flung open the door to room 54, threw several books and a notebook on a bed and let out a long exasperated sigh.

"Where have you been?" asked Jaydee, continuing to drop cards into hands.

"I have just finished my conference with 'The Bone'. One of the two of us is nuts, N-U-T-S, and I can tell you now it is not me."

"All psychology teachers are off their rockers or they wouldn't be psychology teachers," said Elby, arranging her hand.

"You were expecting maybe that you might learn something about human beings in psychology?" asked Mary Ann.

"'The Bone' is the worst. I should ask her as an outsider what she thinks of the human race."

"Three no trump," said Barbara, "Why do y'all call her 'The Bone'?"

"Pass, You don't know how she got that nickname?"

"Four hearts. I thought everybody had heard that story."

"Four no trump. No, I don't and I wish somebody would tell me now. What have you got partner?"

"Well, one day this dog came into the classroom, see? Of course, it disrupted the place. Everybody was giggling and trying to pet the dog. Finally our esteemed teacher kept calling it till it finally followed her out into the hall. When she came back in she said, 'That dog is conditioned to a kind voice. He followed me right out of the room when I spoke to him softly.' Then somebody in the back of the room said in a loud whisper, 'Any dog will follow a bone.' So she's been called 'The Bone' ever since."

"Well, I certainly don't see the need for those conferences," said Jaydee as she placed a card on the trick being played.

"She says it's a way to get to know her students better," said Corky. "What did she ask you, Babe?"

"Probably the same thing she asked you. You were scheduled right after me, weren't you?"

"What?" said Corky. "No, I didn't have any conference with her."

"She told me when I left about 3:25 that you would be in at 3:30. It was on the bulletin board. I went by the Post Office and The Goose before I came back to the dorm. Boy are you going to be late."

"More than that. It's 4:15 now," said Elby.

"I didn't know a thing about a conference," insisted Corky. "How was I supposed to know? She should have told me. I never look at her bulletin board. The last time I did, it had white mice and monkeys."

"You stood up the wrong person," said Jaydee seriously.

"There goes my D average. Do you suppose she is still there?"

"I doubt it, but you'd better go see," said Mary Ann. "Come on, I'll go with you. I want to check my mailbox before supper."

Corky and Mary Ann had walked only about fifty yards from the dorm when Mary Ann gasped, "Look who's coming. 'The Bone' in person."

"Hide me," pleaded Corky. But it was too late.

"Oh, hello, ma'am," said Corky with a big smile. "I am very sorry I wasn't at my conference. I just found out about it a few minutes ago."

"That's perfectly all right," said 'The Bone'. Her voice was cold.

"You failed to come. I had many other important things to do. But I have my revenge. I have written on the bulletin board in red letters for everyone to see, 'This appointment was not kept by Corky'. I am going to leave it up there for a whole week so that everyone may know that you are not a reliable person."

With that statement, she threw out her chin, tilted her head back, and walked rapidly away.

All the gang thought the "revenge" was a scream. Corky could find no humor in it at all.

"You needn't knock yourselves out so," she snapped when we teased her about it. "You aren't flunking the class."

"Her revenge," laughed Elby. "You poor soul, having your name up there in red letters for a whole week."

"At least you don't have to wear them around your neck," commented Babe. "I didn't think psychology teachers were vindictive. Her revenge might prompt you to get your revenge, and then there's no end to it."

"How could I get revenge on her?" asked Corky. "I'd be in worse trouble than I am now."

"Maybe you'll think of something," said Mary Ann.

That evening at the bridge game, the idea of Corky's revenge was discussed further. Several plans were explored. And then someone hit upon the perfect solution.

"Corky, you have got to do it," urged Elby.

"It will rank with Pavlov's dogs in the important events of all psychology," insisted Barbara.

Finally Corky was persuaded to call the Faculty Club, where 'The Bone' resided, and leave a message. The message was that 'The Bone' was to call a certain telephone number and ask if they had a box for her.

That would be Corky's revenge?

We will never know. We will never have the satisfaction of finding out if 'The Bone' called that number and asked if they had a box for her. We will be denied the pleasure of seeing the reaction on her face if she carried out the instructions of the message Corky left. But I still sometimes laugh to myself when I remember that the number we left for her to call was the telephone number of the local funeral home.

CHAPTER ELEVEN

RIMES OF THE NOT-SO-ANCIENT MARINER

THE YEAR 1944 WAS A CREATIVE ONE for me, at least as far as writing poetry, if indeed it can be called that. I lay no claim to the originality of the two para-phrased pieces. I do not know where they came from, but freely admit adopting them to fit the life and times of MSCW circa 1944. They could not be published in or about the 'W' campus or Columbus. Reproductions were not easily come by before the advent of the copying machine.

But I knew some students at Ole Miss who were on the staff of the Ole Miss magazine. Even if I could remember who they were, I would not reveal their names now. *The Rebel* was the avant-garde college publication of its day and eager to print risqué jokes or things likely to ignite controversy. So it was in *The Rebel* that these poems appeared. When copies of the magazine got back to MSCW, they caused quite a stir.

If Dr. Parkinson or any of the faculty or administration ever saw the issues of *The Rebel* which contained these poems, they did not acknowledge the fact.

At the time, the writing was obviously unsigned. If you have copies of those old *Rebel* magazines in your attic, and always wondered who wrote these poems but were afraid to ask, now you know.

MSCW HOW WE LOVE IT!

Now you have heard the story
How the judgment day will be;
And the records will be brought up
And showed to you and me.
Now when Gabriel blows his trumpet
And St. Peter rings his bell;
We'll get a front seat there in heaven

'Cause we've served our hitch in hell.

Yes, we "Messy W" students
From the seniors to the frosh,
Have lived just by the handbook
And all those rules by gosh!
We've "heiled" to deal ole Dr. P.
We've studied oh so well,
And we'll get front seats in heaven
'Cause we've served our hitch in hell.

We've worn our uniform of blue,
We've all been in by ten,
We've had to do with letters, too,
Nine months without our men!
So when we sight those pearly gates
We'll hear St. Peter yell
"Take a front seat here in heaven, girls,
You've served your hitch in hell."

We've seen those failing grades go home,
We often torn our hair;
But in that promised land above,
There'll be no faculty there.
So don't despair my comrades,
Just serve your task here well;
"Cause we'll all get into heaven
We'll have served our hitch in hell.

Spring—1944

"HEIL TO THE CHIEF"
A stranger stood at the gates of hell,
And the devil himself had answered the bell.
He looked him over from head to toe,
And said, "My friend, I'd like to know,
What you have done in the line of sin,
To entitle you to come within."
Then Dr. P. with his usual guile
Stepped forth and flashed his toothy smile.
"When I took charge in '31
The students then were having fun.
When I got in, I soon clamped down
I barely let them go to town.
They wanted to dance with all their heart,
I finally agreed—six inches apart.
To campus them was not enough,
I added '18 weeks' and all that stuff.
In chapel I'd have lots to say
To see how long I could make them stay.
They wanted a nickelodeon in The Goose
With that I'd never turn them loose.
While I was there, they'd not see that day;
Say, what is a nickelodeon anyway?
And after they got tired of me,
I'd let them listen to Mrs. P.
To all the students I was very indomitable
Those without 'B' averages were abominable.
This I did and lots more junk
And blamed it all on Nellie and Unc."*
So B. L. raved both long and loud
And the devil stood and his head he bowed.
He finally said, "Let's make this clear,
You'll have to leave, you can't stay here.
For once you mingle with this mob,

I'd have to hunt myself a job."
—Fall 1944

**Nellie and Unc refer to Dean Nellie Keirn and Eugenia "Unc" Summer, then president of Student Government.*

THE DEATH OF HENRY THE FIFTH, A BALLAD

The crowd was gathered, the night was young.
Merriment prevailed, songs were sung.
But not much later, things were lagging,
Something was missing, the party was sagging.

The gang wound down to their wits end,
Then in came Henry on the arm of a friend.
Now Henry's a friend to have fun with,
And there is no friend like Henry the Fifth.

When he gets with you, you swing and sway,
You love everybody, and you feel sooo gay.
So on this night he was well enjoyed.
All forgot their troubles, no one was annoyed.

When into this merriment, tragedy spread,
Someone discovered that Henry was dead!
Now just who killed him was hard to say,
But we all grieved for Henry when he passed away.

He was loved so dearly, and he served so well,
May he rest in peace, be it heaven or hell.
His cherished memory, we'll not forget,
Oh, the death of Henry, we all regret.

Now you've heard the story, though it's told quite risky,
of the death of Henry, the fifth of whiskey.

CHAPTER TWELVE

THE WEARING OF THE GREEN

IN A "TALE OF TWO CITIES" Charles Dickens wrote: "It was the best of times, it was the worst of times." Certainly the 1940's, like almost any period in history, can be classified as both the best of times and the worst of times. The front fence of MSCW was in a sense our "iron curtain," (though Churchill wouldn't make this a famous phrase until a speech he made in the late forties). Even though the student body of about a thousand was sheltered behind that iron fence on College Street, we were not protected from the news of the war which arrived daily. We did have radios. We listened to stations that played *"There'll be smoke on the water, on the land and the sea, when the Army and the Navy march on to victory."* But victory was still a long way off when we entered the 'W' as freshmen in the fall of 1943. For those who cannot relate to the seriousness of this, consider that, because of the war, the Ole Miss-Mississippi State football game was not played in 1943!

Because of the urgent requirements for materials to be used for war, there were many shortages. In the United States there was rationing of meat, butter, sugar, fats, oils, coffee, canned goods, and gasoline. If you can imagine it, shoes were also rationed. Each family had little books of coupons required for purchasing the rationed goods.

While there was radio news, people really did not know what was going on. The public's right to know is restricted during war. Posters were placed all over reminding citizens that the enemy might be listening. "Loose talk costs live," and "The slip of the lip may sink a ship" read the signs. No one was to discuss the slightest fact that might be overheard and used against the United States.

A newspaper came to the dorm daily, but students seldom had time to read it. We got funny little "V Mail" letters from men in the service. This was a letter written on a special form, which was then reduced in size by a photographic process. This was supposed to expedite the mail. The government set up an Office of Censorship which had the power to censor all communications. Many letters we received ha been "censored," whole lines blacked out. Some had sentences or paragraphs cut out so that pages hung in shreds when removed from their envelopes. We would try to guess where the writer was. Some couples had secret codes, agreed upon earlier, so that whereabouts could be revealed without breaching security.

We got other kinds of news—tragic news—that someone's brother, father, or boyfriend had been killed in action or was missing. A long distance telephone call then was usually the sign of bad news, not today's happy reaching out and touching someone.

On June 6, 1944, just as we were beginning summer vacation, the Allies invaded Europe and the fighting became more intense. Our Christmas present our sophomore year was the Battle of the Bulge, only we didn't know at the time what it was. What we did know was that an awful lot of our friends were "missing in action." Merry Christmas and a Happy New Year! But it was to prove a happy new year after all, peace did come in 1945.

If I could have had my way, I would have been ferrying airplanes to Europe; but they just wouldn't take me in the WAFS (Women's Auxiliary Ferrying Service). I had not lived long enough on this planet at that time, and I had not flown enough hours in an airplane. Otherwise I might today be greeting you from the flight deck of an Eastern Air Lines DC-9: "This is your captain speaking, welcome aboard." On the other hand, I might instead be resting on the bottom of the North Atlantic and not writing memoirs of days at the 'W' at all. As it was, I had to sit out the war in a Piper Cub in the Civil Air Patrol And I couldn't even do that while I was in Columbus.

But we at the MSCW campus did have our ways of serving. In a country always prone to a lot of letter abbreviations, the 'W' offered the VAMS, the VERCS, and the VOWS. The trouble with these letter abbreviations is that forty years later nobody remembers what they stood for. You think I remember? Well, I don't. I only recall that the VOWS were devoted to Red Cross-type activities, rolling bandages, studying first aid and nursing skills—that sort of thing. The VERCS were clerical positions. In all three, the "V" stood, not so much for "victory," though it did that too, but for "Volunteer."

The VAMS were "Volunteer Auxiliary Monitors Service" I think. I know what they did because I did it! There were the folks who brought you your friendly meals in Shattuck Dining Hall. With a war effort, there were not many people who aspired to wait on tables at the 'W' for a living. It was a lot more profitable, respectable, and satisfying to go to Mobile and work in the shipyards or take up aircraft riveting. To solve this problem, the college administration created positions that would now be called "work-study" jobs. Still there were not enough waitresses to serve the large student body in the family-style dining manner. Therefore the students themselves were solicited to help win the war by filling these table-serving positions, called "monitors." Campus leaders, presidents of Student Government, Women's Athletic Association, Civic League, and the four classes, were challenged to be the first to volunteer to set the pattern for the rest of the student body. They accepted the challenge as did a large percentage of the students. One could sign up for a month and receive the exalted salary of $30. Those of you who are mathematical will quickly calculate that monthly allotment figure comes to $1 a day, or 35 cents a meal (we had to round off somewhere, for crying out loud). But it wasn't easy because a month was the minimum time that could be "volunteered." This meant a thirty-day commitment. Fortunately, it was possible to get a substitute to work some meals, or some days, provided the sub had received the proper training in advance. There were always people looking for others to fill their shift at a given meal or on a given day.

A shift in the dining hall consisted of arrival about forty-five minutes prior to the serving of a meal. That got rather early in the morning since the regular breakfast was at 7 a.m. The monitors ate first, then set up two tables which seated eight persons each. The uniform of the monitor was a long white coat. After putting on this garment, the next assignment was to get the linens and silverware for each table. When the 'W' set a table then, as now, it was set correctly. We always had damask table cloths, large cloth napkins, and the proper setting, knife blades turned to the plate, and other silverware laid out in the most formal and proper manner. And there was always some kind of flower or living plant on the table.

One place at the table was for the hostess. Sometimes this seat was assigned to a faculty member or senior, otherwise it was the last chair to be taken. The hostess had to serve the food and exchange the dialogue with the monitor regarding bringing additional food, clearing the dishes and such.

Each monitor was responsible for her two tables and those sixteen people for the entire meal. She traveled to and from the kitchen bringing the entrees, bowls of vegetables, and beverages. Hot coffee was a particularly difficult thing to serve. The "pots" were stainless steel and got very hot. They were heavy, and it took some dexterity to balance a cup and saucer and pour hot coffee from a full pot. When student diners choose to be difficult, and there were those who did so choose, many monitors may have been tempted to pour the hot liquid down their necks; but so far as I know, no one was ever scalded during mealtime.

When the meal was completed, one did not just get up and leave. Students had to sit at the table until the entire group was dismissed by the sounding of the whistle at twenty-five minutes past the hour. Then the monitors had to clear the tables, take all dishes to the kitchen, and pick up the tablecloths and napkins for deposit in the laundry bags. Don't forget now that all this was being done for the lofty sum of 35 cents. While you are remembering that, recall also that 35 cents would buy a ticket to the movies then. When discouragement set in, we were reminded that we were doing our part for the war effort. I'm still not quite sure just how all this won the war.

Like Gaul, all Shattuck Hall was divided into parts, but unlike Gaul, it was four parts, not three. To the far left on entering the hall was the freshman section, next came the sophomores, and on the right side the juniors, and finally the seniors. The 'W' girls were assigned to tables, and a student never sat outside her own class section except by special invitation. Tables were "closed" (not set up on a rotation).If your assigned table was not in service for a meal, you had to go find a place to sit. In spite of the fact that the 'W' has always been a friendly campus, there were times when that was a lonely search.

Then there were the Birthday Dinners. One night a month, Dr. Parkinson entertained all the girls who had birthdays that month by coming to Shattuck and sitting at the birthday tables. Not only was this a "command performance" on the part of the honorees; but had we been in another kind of army, the orders would have still read "full dress uniform." For us that meant Sunday dress, hose, heels, the works. Of course, the reward for attending this celebration in such fine attire was an especially good meal and the questionable treat of being serenaded with a chorus of "Happy Birthday."

Singing was a big part of Shattuck dining even though it was not looked upon favorably by the administration. The wait for dismissal was made more cheerful by the addition of songs. The class divisions made echo singing and class songs popular. The traditional "Stand Up" was often crooned to someone special for some special reason; and near Christmas holidays, sound effects of silverware against glasses made things "jingle all the way." That also brought out the all time dining hall favorite:

"X more days till vacation.
Then we got to the station.
Back to civilization,
The train will carry us there."

This wonderful family-style dining was a way of life at MSCW from 1885 until 1970. It is certainly among MY most cherished memories of the 'W', and that includes the monitoring. In retrospect it was great fun and it is certainly handy to be able to tell my children that "I worked my way through college waiting on tables for thirty-five cents a meal." (They aren't particularly impressed.)

I can't leave the dining hall memories without sharing one last story of a happening in that delightful place. One evening at the dinner meal, I was not "serving", but seated at a table near the swinging doors which separated the dining area from the kitchen. I know some of you remember the enormous crash that echoed across the entire area when a monitor dropped a tray filled with dishes, glasses, silverware or "all of the above." (No, they didn't all get broken. While the supply lasts, the remaining Shattuck Hall dishes may still be purchased at special Homecoming sales.)

This particular night one of the vegetables being served for dinner was spinach, which was not on the hit parade of favorite foods. A moan went up as soon as the girls at the tables near the kitchen doors saw the green-leaf mounds filling the serving dishes coming out on the trays carried by the monitors. The ripple of discontentment rolled across the hall. One girl at my table was particularly vocal about her dislike of spinach, and she protested loudly that it was one thing that should never be offered 'W' students. Just as she was at her most dramatic raving, a monitor came roaring through the doors balancing a tray with two bowls of steaming green spinach. She stepped on something—probably a few drops of water or some other liquid—and skidded across the floor. In her attempt to keep from dropping the serving bowls, she tilted the tray in a great sweeping motion. The bowls stayed on the tray The spinach did not. By some quirk of physics, the entire contents of one bowl came flying out and through the air right to the top of the head of the protesting girl. That certainly kept her from eating the spinach. "Green wig" and all, she retired from the dining hall. We never had spinach after that without laughing and telling the story of "the wearing of the green."

CHAPTER THIRTEEN

"HERE'S TO OUR UNIFORM OF BLUE"

THERE WAS NEVER A SIGN OVER the Old Maid's Gate which read "USN", but MSCW was nevertheless the "navy yard of Mississippi." The college required the wearing of navy blue uniforms from the time it opened until the mid-forties. The Student Handbook (required reading) very definitely and thoroughly stated what was to be worn, when, where and how. The quotes in this chapter are from that handbook, dated 1943-44.

"Every MSCW student is required to wear the prescribed uniform. All students except seniors must leave and return to the campus in uniform. This includes returning to the campus at the opening of the school. The uniform is dark navy blue for school and dark navy blue or white for dress.

Seniors who are leaving the campus may be out of uniform for one hour before the time of their leaving town and one hour after their return, provided they are not seen off the campus out of uniform except as they go through the city on their way to and from bus stations, railroad stations, or destination named in their permits. They are not to stop in town out of uniform.

The school uniform may be of any plain dark navy blue goods. Two-toned materials and material flecked with gray or other colors are not in uniform."

As pointed out in an earlier chapter, navy blue clothing was not easily found in war-rationed shopping. At best wardrobes were limited. Many students had to dye clothes navy blue to get even a few outfits. The result was twofold. One, upon each washing (by the MSCW laundry), the garment got lighter, until it finally became a tattle-tale gray color. Two, the navy blue dye which did not come out in the laundry rubbed off on the skin of the wearer of the dyed clothing. Some girls went through the entire year with a blueish cast on their bodies.

"Dark navy blue one-piece dresses, trimmings and facings must be blue or black, dark navy blue blouses and skirts or dark navy coat suits may be worn.

Coats must be of solid white material, or of dark navy blue material trimmed with blue, or black. Fur as a trimming or separate piece is not allowed. Short uniform sports coats with colored lining may be worn on the campus only. Colored linings in full length coats are out of uniform. White coats and sweaters may be worn only for warmth and therefore must have long sleeves. If a white slipover sweater is worn, it must be worn over a blue blouse with blue collar showing at the neck of the sweater."

We found a wonderful answer to the short uniform sports coats. Every student who knew anyone connected with the Navy got that person to get them a Navy Pea Jacket. They were warm, they were Navy "navy blue" and they made us feel rather special. We could have denim pants, which at that time weren't called "blue jeans", but we could only wear them in the dorms—never out on campus.

Our "white slipover sweater" became a long-sleeved white sweatshirt complete with the required navy-blue collar. Since being out of uniform resulted in a week's "campus", we paid strict attention to these uniform regulations. How was it enforced? MSCW had an HONOR CODE which read:

"The honor system is based on the principle of individual responsibility and personal honor. It applies to every phase of college life. The Honor System requires that each individual shall make it her personal responsibility to report all infringements of the honor code."

"Socks of any color may be worn with both blue and white uniform on the campus. Socks may not be worn with high heeled shoes."

The wearing of colored socks gave students the opportunity to produce some of the loudest color combinations ever seen on the 'W' campus. There were reds and greens, purples, plaids and stripes. Not being able to wear them with high heeled shoes never posed any great unhappiness as far as I know.

"After campus limits, six and seven o'clock, stockings must be worn to the Gilmer Hotel Coffee Shop and dining room and to the Bell Café.. Woolen gloves of any color may be worn on the campus at any time and off the campus at any time except Sunday.

Scarves may be of two types—blue and white. Blue scarves may be worn at any time with either navy or white uniforms. White scarves may be worn under the same regulations as white uniforms. Colored scarves may be worn with raincoats on rainy days.

Scarves on the hair may not be worn off the campus, or when dress uniform is required. Scarves may not be worn on the hair on Sunday after 10:30 a.m. even with a raincoat.

Scarves or hats must completely cover all curling devices, including bobby pins when these are worn outside of the dormitory, in the dining room, or in the parlors of the dormitories."

Ah, the scarves! What a multitude of sins they covered. For that matter the raincoats did, too. Like socks, raincoats could be of any color, though we were reminded reversible raincoats must always be worn with the raincoat side out. It was a common practice to go to breakfast in pajamas wearing a raincoat over them. Often the rolled-up leg of the PJs would slip down below the raincoat sending the wearer scurrying to a corner or behind a post to hitch up the problem. Hair was rolled, and tucked under the scarf, except for that Sunday regulation. Because full dress uniforms were required on Sunday after 10:30 a.m. and since scarves could not be worn, not even with raincoats, many people never came out of the dorms on Sunday.

"The uniform hat is black or dark navy blue, self-trimmed or trimmed with an ornament, a bunch of flowers, bow or ribbon, or a colored band around the crown only. White hats may also be trimmed with one small ornament or one bunch of flowers, or a colored band around the crown. Colored veils and colored streamers are not allowed.

Hats must be worn to church, to shopping districts, to the hotels, cafes, and restaurants for meals.

Hose must match or blend. While low heels are recommended, a higher heel may be worn for dress. High heels may be worn to class only when a student is leaving immediately after class for an out of town trip or to do student teaching."

What all that is saying, simply, is that a student had to wear a hat and stockings to town every time she went! We had no cars so you can believe we walked to town in hose and LOW HEELS. We also rode bicycles to town most of the time. That's fun in hose and heels! We read the regulations on hats carefully and then turned to the military again. There was a Navy Nurse's overseas cap that met the letter of the law, so many of us had one of them. We could wear "colored bows two inches in width with absolutely no streamers and small artificial flowers in the hair."

Dress uniforms had to be worn "to town, to church, to all public gatherings on the campus including formal recitals, lyceums, birthday dinners, major plays, formal lectures and dance programs." and, as stated before, dress uniforms were required on campus after 10:30 a.m.which meant they had to be worn to the Sunday noon meal.

"The blue dress uniform may be worn on all dress occasions throughout the year. The white dress uniform may be worn for dress and to class after 4 p.m. from the opening of school to November 1 and between April 1 and the close of the school year. Between November 1 and April 1, the white dress uniform may be worn, if desired, after 5 p.m."

The wearing of Class Collars was a fun part of the uniform. There was much tradition in passing down collars from class to class. Here's how you could tell what class a student belonged to by the collar she wore.

"Class collars: Sophomores may wear dark navy collars and

cuffs trimmed with white. The white trimming must be sewed on the navy blue collar and cuffs.

Juniors may wear white collars and cuffs trimmed with dark navy blue. The blue trimming must appear on the back as well as the front and cannot consist only of blue edging. The navy blue must be sewed on the white collars. With suits Juniors may wear white blouses with Junior collars, provided the coat is always kept on.

Seniors may wear white collars and cuffs, white scarves, white fichus or white fronts. With navy blue suits seniors may wear white blouses provided the coat is always kept on."

Can anyone who ever wore one forget the tank suits required for swimming? They were not navy, but royal blue, made of cotton, and one size did not fit anyone. If you think they looked bad dry, you should have seen them wet!

Gym suits were navy shorts and white blouses. They could not be worn on front campus at all, and the handbook said, "Students may not loiter in The Goose in gym suits"—that meant we could stay only fifteen minutes between 8 a.m. and 6 p.m. Since the gym suits could only be worn in the gym and on the playing field—or going to or from those places—we were always in the process of going to some athletic activity. We used to wear the gym shorts under the navy pea jackets, which were just long enough to cover the shorts and leave a lot of legs sticking out. That was the most daring outfit on campus, but it was "legal."

The last year the uniform was required was the 1944-45 school session. There had been a movement to drop the regulation for several years, but nothing was done about it because of the war. When peace came in the summer of 1945, the men came out of uniform and so did the 'W' girls. When school opened in the fall of 1945, one of the longest and most interesting chapters of 'W' history was closed.

CHAPTER FOURTEEN

HOME SWEET DORM

ASK A 'W' GIRL WHAT SHE REMEMBERS most about dorms and the number of different answers you receive will equal the number of girls you ask. The dorm is home from one to four years; and strong feelings, sentiment, and attachments are formed—not for the four walls as such, of course, but for the people who live within those buildings. The dorm becomes a sanctuary, and it was there we took our joys and our sorrows to be shared with the most important single aspect of college life—friends. We were together with mutual challenges and problems and here we exchanged thoughts, ideas, feelings, and love.

Before anyone thought up the eight-by-ten room with connecting bath and called it a suite, dorms had "room and path"—path down the hall to community facilities. It isn't such a bad arrangement, weighed against the roommate, or suitemate, who barricades herself in the suite's john and leaves others waiting for hours. Someone said, "You've never really lived with anyone until you share the bathroom." There is a lot to share when the whole end of the hall is involved.

In the older 'W' dorms rooms have wash basins, with showers and bathtubs and toilet stalls down the hall. There were some dorms with only showers which gave many 'W' girls occasion to shock home folks by announcing that they 'hadn't had a bath' since they went to the 'W'. With one basin in a room and three girls, there were some interesting situations. Not only does this require exact timing for each person to get her face washed between 6:55 a.m. and 7:00 a.m. breakfast (who got up with the twenty-till whistle?), but it was necessary to remember the color of one's toothbrush. When we arrived my freshman year, all three of us had red toothbrushes. We went home for Thanksgiving reminding each other to purchase new ones. We all came back with blue ones.

Once again at Christmas, we vowed to solve this problem. When we returned for a second semester, not only did each of us have a yellow toothbrush, but that was the color brought by two sophomore visitors who came to spend the night the first weekend we got back. Brushing time that Saturday night became such a comedy of errors that we formed a "Yellow Toothbrush Club", and to this day, in my family of five, guess who has the yellow toothbrush?

Human nature doesn't change much. The pre-freshman girl thinks the dorm room window size is the most important thing in her life. Curtains and bedspreads must match, and freshmen girls worry the entire summer before entering college about whether their room will be right. By the senior year horizons have broadened, along with a few other things, and rooms become real reflections of the personalities who inhabit them. Various articles of sentiment are handed down from one class to another. Plastic milk crates have replaced the wooden orange boxes we used, but creative talents still come up with an amazing number of different ways to use them. Pictures, posters, and other wall hangings were put up in spite of regulations. Someday someone will write an article on "1001 Ways to Arrange Beds in College Dorm Rooms", but they will all have been tried already. One of the first is to put two beds together making one king-sized for three sleepers (more correctly, two sleepers for the one in the middle keeps falling through the crack in the mattress). Beds were turned into double-deck bunks, put L-shaped in corners, or simply moved about the rooms at regular intervals. Anytime dorm life got boring, things could be livened up by changing the room, or by short-sheeting the beds of everyone who had gone away for the weekend.

One universal memory-maker of dorm life might be called "late night capers." Everything from popping corn, preparing feasts of all descriptions, and thinking up daring things to do have made night life in college dorms popular through the years.

Calloway as a freshman residency was the first experience of college living for many 'W' girls. Oldest dorm as well as first building on the front campus, Calloway was built in 1860 for Columbus Female Institute. The Victorian Gothic building was deeded, along with other property, to Industrial Institute and College when the original charter was drawn on March 12, 1884.

All the front campus made up "freshman row" in the forties. Columbus Hall, built in 1896 by the citizens of Columbus, and Hastings, built in 1900 (named for Olivia Hastings), are both in the Queen Ann style of architecture, and all housed the freshman class. One of the nicest things about adjoining buildings was the fact that a person could go from one to the other through connecting doors and never go outside. That gave the class a special unity.

During the World War II years, Calloway had a siren on top of it for air raid drills. There was total blackout when the alarm sounded, and students had to sit in the halls until the "raid" was over, sometimes an hour or more. Often planes from Columbus Air Base would do a fly-by to see if the black out was effective, and there was always someone who wondered if these planes were enemy ones. We didn't really think so, but it was till scary. We accepted these practices without questioning. We were required to do a lot of things differently because our country was at war, but patriotism was probably at the highest level of the twentieth century during World War II.

Living in the dorm provides the opportunity to do many fun things and to come up with a lot of jokes and tricks. During our freshman year, a nearby bakery sold $1 birthday cakes with thick icing decorations, including the name of the honoree. The cake was put into a box for walking it back to the dorm and the top of the box covered with a clear wrap. We called it cellophane then—today we would say plastic wrap. Birthday parties were one of the most frequent of the late night capers. And the bakery sold a lot of these cakes.

We found another use for the clear wrap. Just before lights out, we would take it into a toilet stall in the bathroom. The large sheet of cellophane was slipped between the wooden seat and the ceramic bowl, and pulled tight. For the trick to work, darkness was needed, so we climbed up and unscrewed the bathroom's ceiling light bulb. The rest was waiting—waiting for some unsuspecting girl to come in, flip the light switch several times, give that up and finally go on into the stall. The window of our room, Calloway 62, was at a right angle to the bathroom window, enabling us to hear all the choice remarks from the victim when the trap was sprung. You just wouldn't have expected 'W' girls to have such vocabularies.

After the birthday parties, we found another use for the birthday candles. Girls, usually biology freaks, would go out on campus and find those big, harmless hard-shelled beetles. They would bring them in the dorms in boxes, put the candles on their backs and race them down the halls. The beetles weren't hurt, but the sport did not gain much popularity. Too many girls screamed at the sight of the bugs, and I suppose it was a fire hazard.

In the forties cooking in the dorms presented a creative challenge. There were the usual regulations including some dorms which could not have any electrical appliances at all. Our "ice box" was the space outside our room window, between the glass and the screen. There we stored soft drinks, milk (slipped from the dining hall), and fruit. The temperature of our facility was not very constant. It certainly worked best in winter. There were times when the drinks froze out there, and other times when the screens became unlatched and the bottles fell two or three floors to the ground.

Every so often someone would suggest making chocolate fudge. Trying to cook it on the bottom of an iron leaves much to be desired—fully cooked fudge among other things. There was a story circulating that fudge could be cooked with the heat from a light bulb, but I didn't believe anyone ever went that far.

Uncooked lemon "icebox" pies were easier to make, if someone could come up with a can of "Dime Brand" condensed milk, so called because it really cost ten cents. Sugar was rationed, and as hard to come by as was a Hershey chocolate bar. Whenever either was received by retailers, a crowd gathered quickly and soon all was sold out.

(Any time during the early forties when a line was seen forming at The Goose, it meant one small box of candy had come in. About the time the word was out, so was the candy.)

We made a lemon pie one afternoon, intending to eat it after study hour that night. We didn't want the whole end of the hall to know because there wasn't that much to share. When we finished making the pie, we hid it in my closet. During the afternoon my roommate, who did not know about the pie, let alone where it was hidden, came in and tossed a few things about. That night we opened the closet door to get our treat. Right in the middle of the beautiful lemon pie was a dirty saddle oxford that looked as big as a battleship. So much for cooking—or uncooking—in the rooms.

One night when we were sophomores in Reneau, one of my friends on the hall, Marianne Stroble, went to take a bath. My roommate, Lola Beth Deavers, two other people on the floor, and I were in the mood for mischief. We waited until Marianne had time to settle down in her hot tub of water. Reneau was one of the dorms that did have tubs. We slipped into the adjoining shower stall, peeped over the wall and saw that her back was to us. Good! We poured the entire contents of a bottle of red ink into the water behind her. She continued singing and splashing away. We had thought to make her get out and run her bath again. And that was one result. We had not counted on her blood curdling scream which would be heard three floors as she yelled, "My God, I've amputated my leg."

Have you heard it said that you always remember where you were when some earth-shaking event took place? I was in front of Reneau playing softball when someone called from the window that President Roosevelt had died. The date was April 12, 1945.

The campus and the nation mourned the dead president who had only recently returned from the Yalta Conference with Churchill and Stalin. One of Roosevelt's greatest admirers was Miss Pohl who had been so pleased by his decisive win over Thomas E. Dewey for his fourth term.

The great victory that Roosevelt did not live to see came less than a month later. On May 8, 1945 the free world celebrated V-E Day, Victory in Europe. Again I was playing softball in front of Reneau. The radio reported wild celebrating at Times Square in New York City. The 'W' campus reacted more sedately. There was still the war in the Pacific; but for the first time since 1941, there was hope that the end of World War II was a possibility. More than a million men who had been drafted, plus the others who were serving in the Armed Forces, might get home in time to go to college with us.

Victory came during summer vacation of 1945 and we were not on the 'W' campus. The forties were halfway gone, and thankfully the last half of the decade would be a time of peace.

We had a lot of time together in the dorms, because aside from classes and meals, we had little to do. There were a great many rules about leaving campus, as you can see in that chapter. The long hours of being together gave us time to make friendships that were meaningful and lasting. We had bridge games, listened to the radio and records, talked, and studied together.

After the original freshmen dorm assignments, roommates usually found each other by mutual interests. Also after freshman year, rooms were assigned by scholastic averages. The girl with the highest grades got her choice of rooms in the next level dorm. Corner rooms usually went first. In order to get one, it was necessary to have a high average or a smart roommate. Wonder what ever happened to that custom?

We had a core of die-hard, outdoor-minded athletes who slept all year up on the sleeping porches of Peyton, Fant, and Reneau. The steam plant at the 'W' has always provided comfortable dorms—sometimes too warm for sleeping. The fresh-air gang trudged up to sleep in the elements even in rainy or below freezing weather. It worked. I slept up there all my sophomore year and never even had a cold.

One of the oldest and most unique traditions of dorm life has been observed for many years at the 'W', and only at the 'W' as far as anyone knows. A towel hung over the door of a dormitory room means "Do Not Disturb." This law has been universally respected by 'W' students with the result that there is greater privacy when requested and a better environment for studying than in any other college or university in the country.

If home is where the heart is, then the center of college memories will always return to the dorms and to the people with whom we spent some of the best years of our lives.

SLEEPERS AWAKE!

Breaker of each dream
Bringer of reality.
Bundle of steam
Hated by morality.
Shattering the stillness
Ill-fated missile
Oh get thee hence
Twenty till whistle

—Margaret Boland, October 1944

CHAPTER FIFTEEN

ONE IF BY LAND, TWO IF BY RAIL

FOR REASONS KNOWN NOW ONLY to God and Dr. Parkinson, Christmas holidays (Spring, too, for that matter) began at one minute past midnight. A school which was so strict about students returning before 10 p.m. certainly picked a strange time to dismiss. The three train possibilities did not leave until well into the next day, and since we had no cars in which to travel home, most students rode charter busses which departed promptly at 12:01 a.m. Whatever else I remember about riding them, the most outstanding fact was how cold the weather usually was and the inside of the busses wasn't much better. We had to sit around in the dorms from after supper until time to go. Of course no one was going to sleep. Finally, at the stroke of twelve, we could go over and board the vehicles which were parked in the street by the gym. They would be lined up ready to spread in all directions, and students had to locate the one going in their direction and get in the scramble for seats. During the war, standing on busses for long distances was not at all unusual.

We met classes on Monday, Wednesday, and Friday; and Tuesday, Thursday AND SATURDAY. Most everyone got out by mid-afternoon, but we still had to wait. Why not cut class and leave early? There were DOUBLE CUTS for any class missed for whatever reason the day before and the day following holidays. Being present in class was so very serious that everyone was expected to be present unless lying in state at the local mortuary.

As you read a few chapters ago, students had to leave and return to the campus in full uniform. Busses didn't have rest rooms on board then. On trips departing Columbus, there was mass exodus to the ladies room the first time the bus topped. Once outside the five mile limit, we were "free"; and during that ten minute rest stop, the 'W' girls managed to get out of their navy blue uniforms and into "civilian clothes."

At the slow wartime speeds, the Christmas charters took three hours to make the 88 mile trip to Meridian, putting us there in the very wee hours of the morning. We always looked forward to going straight to Weidmann's Café, which stayed open 24 hours, and ordering hot coffee and their famous Black Bottom Pie.

Travel by rail made getting in and out of uniform easier because on board the train, there were more and better dressing rooms. The reverse change had to be made on the return to Columbus, when colorful outfits were exchanged for uniforms as the students neared the MSCW limits.

Two mainline railroads served the needs of students. The Frisco from Memphis heading southeast to the Tombigbee shores gathered students from intermediate stops across the northern half of Mississippi. The GM&O Rebel originated in Mobile, came up through Alabama to Meridian. Girls got on up and down the line, sometimes driving some distance to the station. The Rebel continued northward toward the "O"of the Gulf, Mobile, and Ohio railroad, but it did not stop in Columbus. Instead, girls bound for the 'W' had to get off at Artesia, some eighteen miles to the west, and take a bus (provided by the railroad), from Artesia to the campus.

The Columbus and Greenville Railroad came within a block of MSCW, coming across the state from the Delta. As each of these rail lines got closer to Columbus, their cars were filled more and more with 'W' students. Returning to school from a holiday wasn't so bad when friends were boarding all the way along the journey and visiting and catching up could take place.

Bicycles were a very popular form of transportation at MSCW. Unless you have lived without a car, you cannot fully appreciate the value of these two-wheeled marvels. We all had big, heavy-frame, "fat-tire" bikes with just one speed, but they served us well. They made it much easier to get to class and to town. We used to go on long bike hikes on Saturday afternoons, including out to Lake Norris on Saturdays—a very pretty spot that was off limits. Reneau was the farthest dorm from the dining hall, post office, and The Goose. It is now almost the center point of the campus, but then Shattuck is no longer the dining spot, nor is the post office in the basement of Hastings. Many times, students would leave bicycles when they left MSCW for good. It was either too much trouble to take them home, or they did not anticipate any further need for them. There are still a few of the old-fashioned bikes around campus that must date back to that era of cycling.

We had a visitor one weekend who heard us talking about being in certain clubs. We let her wonder awhile, and then told her that "Motor Boat" was not an aquatic society, but our take off on "Mortar Board", "Flashlight" was the sophomore honor society, Lantern, and "Match"the junior group, Torch.

We had visitors such as one musician who was performing a lyceum (that's what they called the cultural programs) and took his own grand piano on concert tour, shipping it by rail freight. His agent caused quite a stir in the Columbus Western Union office when he sent the following telegram: BODY IS HERE BUT LEGS CANNOT BE LOCATED.

CHAPTER SIXTEEN

RULES ARE FOR WHEN YOU RUN OUT OF BRAINS

MSCW HAD A REPUTATION, which it richly deserved, for being "very strict", and the many rules and regulations caused much unhappiness, a great deal of griping, and much planning on how to get by without observing them or how to get rid of them. I spent the better part of several nights reading the Student Government Handbooks for 1943-44 and 44-45. I laughed till I cried over some of the material. I laughed because the rules seem so archaic and funny when we read them in the "high tech" year of 1983. I suppose I cried because the social changes which the past forty years have wrought probably deserve some tears from somebody.

The authority figures in our lives at the 'W' during the forties were the president, Dr. Burney L. Parkinson, and the dean, Miss Nellie S. Keirn. But by and large the students were governed by the Student Handbook. The 1943-44 handbook has 102 printed pages. (The 1982-83 handbook has 43 pages, including a lot of pictures—so much for progress.)

A message from President Parkinson begins the book: "here is an environment in which you may grow physically, intellectually, socially, and spiritually. Here former students and faculty have created for you a spirit of democracy, courtesy, friendliness, consideration for others, industry and good sportsmanship. This heritage is yours to utilize and to perpetuate. Here every minute is fraught with opportunity for her who understands, appreciates and harmonizes with her environment."

It is not the purpose of this memoir, nor is it within the scope of this book, to review the entire student handbook; but we will try to give the reader a brief summary of what life was like living under the code of '43-44-45, trying to "harmonize with the environment."

It becomes necessary to define some terms. A reprimand was the punishment for minor infractions such as "undue noise, keeping light on or being up overtime, failure to observe study hour."

Two reprimands was a "campus" which meant: "except to attend church on Sunday morning, one may not leave the campus; and one may not have dates."

Campusment was the penalty for such things as: "dishonesty in all academic work, misrepresentation of act, theft or dishonest use of property of others, riding or leaving the campus with men without a chaperone and without permission at night; drinking, or the possession of any alcoholic beverage, any offense which brought reproach upon the college, or that was a breach of the honor system."

The rules regarding dating and leaving the campus probably resulted in the longest and most severe punishments. There were people who had six weeks "campus," and a few who had 18 weeks! This was an entire semester of staying within the 42 acres, with no social life with the opposite sex.

The resentment was particularly bitter when such campusment occurred because some student defied authority and met a boyfriend on leave—one who was often about to go overseas. To most students the rules seemed harsh and unreasonable, and it did appear that whoever wrote them had run out of brains. Thus in many situations, 'W' girls decided dates were hard enough to come by and would slip out and meet men.

Many parents chose the 'W' for their daughters because of the strict supervision, often more strict than the girls had at home. Students made proposals for revisions of rules through designated Student Government channels, but changes came slowly. Little did we know that the World War II years were the beginning of the end of the Victorian customs.

All students had to be in class unless they were in the infirmary. "A student present at chapel but not in her own seat will be considered absent." One unexcused class or chapel absence, one reprimand—the second, a week's campusment.

Are you ready for this? "There are SIX registers in each dormitory, namely: registers for: 1)leaving the campus to go within the city limits, 2) leaving the city, 3) going to the college hospital, 4) for dates, 5) for guests, and 6) for spending the night out (in another campus dorm)."

Students had to sign out and sign in. Signing for another was one of the "serious offenses."

Civic League inspected rooms daily except Sunday. The grading system was as follows:

Floors unswept	20
Floors poorly swept	10
Beds unmade	20
Beds poorly made	10
Dirty lavatory	15
Untidy table	5
Untidy dresser, etc	10
Wastebasket half full or with food	10
Clothes about room	5
Failure to dust properly	5
Unclean window sills	5
Bottles, dishes, trash in window.	10
Unclean closets	15
Unclean dishes anywhere in room	10
General disorder	10

When the total reached 125, a reprimand was given to everyone living in the room. Sweeping trash into the hall brought an automatic "rep."

Freshmen had lights out at 10:30 p.m. every night except Saturday when they could stay up till 11 p. m. Sophomores had an 11 p.m. turn off except for 11:30 on Saturday. Juniors and seniors could stay up till midnight.

Students could smoke only if they had written permission from their parents and only then in special places—their own room in fireproof dorms (Fant, Peyton, and Reneau), and in "smoking rooms" in other dorms. Students with permits had to get further permission from the social adviser of any dorm they visited.

"The penalty for violation of the smoking regulation is one to four weeks' campusment."

Quiet had to be observed by members of all classes during study hour (7-9:30 p.m.), during "Meditation" on Sunday (2-2:30 p.m.), from 8 a.m. to 4 p.m. during the day, and from 10 p.m. to 6 a.m.

Radios had to be registered with the social adviser and could not be moved from the room for which they were registered. ("All record players on which the volume can be controlled will be considered as radios.") If they were heard outside the room where they were playing, they were taken up and held by the social adviser until the semester ended or the owner took them home. Students in the rooms above or below could complain if they heard radios with the same result.

"When roommates are not in accord as to when and in what volume the radio in their room is to be played, the wishes of the student desiring quiet shall prevail."

Can you imagine what just one stereo system would have done to that environment?

There could be no visiting between rooms during closed study hour or during Sunday meditation. Each student had one permit per semester to leave the college and the city of Columbus from Friday noon to Sunday night. No permits were issued from the beginning of school in September till the third weekend of October. This meant nearly six weeks on campus before going home and was doubtless a factor in some of the severe freshmen homesickness during the period.

Before leaving the college for a trip out of town, each student had to fill out a "pink slip" with all the trip data. Failure to do this was one week's campusment.Visiting a day or less in nearby towns had to meet these conditions: "1. Permission from home. 2. With dates—chaperonage by faculty, parents, grandparents, older sister, uncles, or aunts. 3. Without dates—chaperonage by parents, grandparents, older sisters, older brothers, uncles, aunts, other MSCW parents."

A lot of long campusments resulted from "extension of permits." The first day was a week's campus, and only death or serious illness in the family was an acceptable excuse for not returning to MSCW on time from any visit away. The handbook plainly stated there was to be no treatment of eyes, teeth, or physical examinations without advance notice to the college physician and the dean PRIOR to leaving the campus!

"Students returning to the campus in automobiles must be on the campus by 6 p.m. in winter or 7 p.m. in fall or spring if unchaperoned, and by 10 p.m. if chaperoned. The penalty for violation of this regulation is one week's campusment."

Any trip the least out of the ordinary had to be cleared with Dean Keirn. The only time I ever went to see her was on a dare. I had no request, but I patently waited my turn to get in her office. When she asked what I wanted, I stated, "Nothing, Dean Keirn, but I have been on this campus three months and we have not formally met, so I wanted to introduce myself to you." I don't think that had ever happened to her. She was visibly surprised, and if I had ever had a request, I think she would probably have granted it.

I remember another funny story about Dean Keirn. Mississippi State boys came to the 'W' in spite of the dating rules, and there were cadets from the Columbus "Army Air Corps" Base (it became the Air Force later). With no cars being manufactured, gas rationed, and the 'W' requirements for chaperones for dating, most couples stayed on campus. They could "stroll" in certain areas.

In late winter of '44 there were some beautiful weekends. (For a wonder it wasn't raining that Columbus rain.) One Sunday night after the dorms closed, a dorm meeting was called. Our social adviser stated she had a message from Dean Keirn.

"Girls," the dean says, "Something must be done about what is taking place on this campus. I walk around on the weekends and behind every bush there is a couple. What are we going to do when spring really comes?"

"Plant more bushes," said a voice in the back of the room.

After we had read the chaperonage rules, I asked my daughter, who graduated from the 'W' in 1980, to summarize them.

"Seniors may have seven dates a week if they talk to gentlemen uptown no longer than ten minutes Monday through Friday until 5 p.m. with permission from their social adviser, provided they are in groups of two students and one or two men and if a faculty chaperon is with them if it is at night and so long as they ride five people in a five passenger car unless they are riding with a parent or a mature relative closer than a cousin."

That is just the beginning. Freshmen could only go to town in the afternoon three times a week. Sophomores could not go in the morning either, but could go any afternoon. Freshmen and sophomores had to get a "senior chaperone" to go to the movies at night, and could go only three nights. In order to leave campus with dates, they had to have "their own parents or mature relatives closer than cousin."

"Any student whose parents object may not have gentlemen callers."

"Young men may join students at tables in drug stores for not more than fifteen minutes."

"Resident students are not allowed to maintain automobiles."

"Students are not to sit or lie on the ground of the front campus."

"When en route to or from town in the daytime, students may accept rides only with ladies or married couples."

"From Monday through Friday afternoon freshmen may ride without dates in automobiles until 5 p.m. unchaperoned. They must not ride longer than an hour. They must not ride over the

Tombigbee Bridge or more than five miles in any other direction. Faculty chaperonage or chaperonage by parents or mature relatives closer than cousin is required for riding at night. On Saturday and Sunday a freshman may ride only with her parents, or those of some other MSCW student or a faculty member."

"No young man will be permitted to come to a dormitory to have a date unless a date with a definite girl has been arranged in advance and the social adviser informed."

"There are to be no deliveries of any food on Sunday. After 6 p.m. there are to be no deliveries of soft drinks, ice cream, or food of any kind on the campus."

Now for the good news! No student could practice in Music Hall before 7 a.m. during the week. On Sunday students could not sing or play an instrument before 12 noon or during meditation hour.

There are many, many more. We protested, and we broke rules just for the sake of breaking them because it made us feel better somehow. Very few were sorry they broke the rules; they were only sorry they got caught. Some girls transferred to other schools rather than return to some of the long campusments which were carried over to future semesters. Somehow we all lived through this sheltered, protected time in our lives and are no worse off for having experienced it.

But the war was ending and with it would go the old way of life. Men who had fought for a new world and women who had waited on the home fronts while they did so were about to accelerate dramatic changes that would shake the society we had known to its very roots. And so they did, and the old order passed.

CHAPTER SEVENTEEN

I WISH THEY STILL HAD

THE POST OFFICE IN THE BASEMENT of Hastings Hall and the simple, meaningful Morning Watch right after breakfast, a five-minute student led service with participants standing.

Little Southern Café hamburgers—what a lot for the money and what a flavor, before the introduction of styro-foam meat patties.

The Golden Goose Tea Room, the real Goose, with five cent Cokes and doughnuts.

Family-style meals in Shattuck Hall with eight places at the table and formal place settings.

Thirty-five cent movies with real plots and believable characters.

Oh well, I guess we'll always have "Casablanca" on the late show.

Pancakes for breakfast on Sunday morning in Shattuck.

Real bicycles with heavy frames and fat tires, not spider wheels and 100 gears.

That ice cream shop on College Street with malts and sundaes for fifteen cents.

Auctions of the lost and found articles, up by the front fountain, at the end of the school year.

Zouave.

The Blue Serenaders.

Math teachers like Mr. Grossnickle—science teachers like "Teacher" Ferguson.

Field hockey.

The Rebel, the Frisco, and the C & G trains.

Freshman Row with Calloway, Columbus, and Hastings full.

Parking places.

The Rose Garden back by the Little Mississippi.

Someone who dared to dive from the stands in the old gym into the swimming pool.

The Gilmer Hotel.

The Bell Café.

The clicking typewriters in old Industrial Hall.

The big hackberry tree on the front campus which was destroyed in a storm.

Shady clay tennis courts, with the sound of students practicing in nearby Music Hall.

The Honor Code.

CHAPTER EIGHTEEN

THE SPIRIT ENDURES . . . .

THE HISTORIAN GIBBON WARNED against what he called the universal tendency to exalt the past and to deprecate the present. Upon that note it is perhaps best to terminate this set of memories. We have to stop somewhere though doubtless there are hundreds, even thousands, more stories out there that could have been included. We have tried to recall the simple and amusing things. Still time tends to distort our vantage point. and our Creator has wisely endowed us with a nature that remembers the good things as being better.

Most of all I want to leave the thought that the 'W' is alive and well in Columbus, Mississippi. It has continued through war and pestilence, good times and depressions; it has been attacked from within and without and still it has survived for one hundred years. MUW must continue to grow and serve. Young women of today need the 'W' even more than those first students did a century ago. We must all remember what the 'W' has given to us and strive to provide to young women of the future that same opportunity of a tradition of education for women in their own special environment.

Girls and women into the fourth and fifth generation have passed through the classes of II & C, MSCW, and MUW. Hundreds and thousands of 'W' girls have gone into the world to leave distinguished marks in fields of science, medicine, advertising, literature, education, economics, athletics, marketing, theater, home economics, business, technology, law, and government. In addition to all these careers, the largest and perhaps the greatest contribution of women educated at the 'W', has been their roles of wives and mothers. The achievements accomplished by the women educated at this institution have truly been outstanding and unique in the state, the country, and the world.

The Mississippi Legislature in 1884 had the wisdom and the foresight to establish the nation's first state-supported college exclusively for women. Our state's leadership guided the change from II & C to MSCW in 1920 and to university status in 1974. It took a Supreme Court edict to admit men to the student body in 1982. So be it. The 'W' may change the men who attend, but the men will not change the 'W'.

The 'W' has had a century of excellence because of her extraordinary intangible, indescribable spirit. Mississippians respect and cherish tradition, and just as the Legislature of 1884 had the wisdom to establish this great school, the Legislature of 1984, the Board of Trustees for Institutions of Higher Learning, and the people of Mississippi will make sure the state keeps one of the most outstanding traditions it has ever had.

"What unites MSCW?" asks the foreword of the 1945 MEH LADY. Amanda Bridgforth, editor of that yearbook, probably wrote that introduction. How beautifully she phrases the balance of her thought:

"What is this spirit that hovers over our community of lazily-spaced buildings, soaked in prolonged Columbus rains, with glittering window panes that reflect warm Southern lights? What is this spirit that binds together so firmly our navy blue medley of assorted individuals, yet is itself so intangible? MSCW's history is brilliant with girls who wondered at this spirit—who sought to define its poignancy. We wonder now—perhaps we always shall."

And so, above all, this spirit of the 'W' abides. It has been a part of this campus since the first young lady came through that original classroom door. It has danced across the Whitfield stage, dropped through a basketball hoop. That spirit has been lifted in song, carried in the Magnolia Chain, lingered under the Gingko tree, and caught a ride on the sound of the steam whistle. We cannot define it now any more than other generations have been able to say what it is, but it is there. We all still wonder. No doubt we always will.

THE VIEW FROM 2005

When *Be Good Sweet Maid* was first published in 1983 as part of the 100th Anniversary of this wonderful institution, the response was amazing. The book sold copy after copy not only to 'W' students, family, and friends, but to those who held allegiance to other universities, those who lived in other parts of the country, and to students in classes before the forties and many generations after that period.

The overall consensus seemed to be, "We did things like that when I was in college, or very similar things."

If on these few pages we have stirred memories and invoked nostalgia, it has all been worth while.

Many changes have come through the years since this book was first published, and yet it continues to sell well into the second printing. Men now make up a part of the student body, the age of technology is in every building, new classes and majors have been added in a wide variety of fields, interscholastic athletics for women have come-and sadly gone.

Floods, tornados, freezes and heat waves have destroyed buildings and wrecked havoc, but the 'W' is not bricks and mortar, it is spirit.

And the spirit of the 'W' lives on. May she continue to grow and spread light and learning until someone else steps out from the long blue line to write memoirs of the Two Hundredth Anniversary.

ABOUT THE AUTHOR

MARGARET BOLAND ELLIS, who has been known as "Bo" most of her life, was born in Meridian, Mississippi.

After her college years, she worked for Eastern Air Lines and in newspaper and public relations work. She directed the summer camp for the Deep South Girl Scout Council and coached and taught high school algebra and journalism at St. Paul's Episcopal School in Mobile. She has also taught creative writing at the University of South Alabama.

The first woman Little League manager in the state of Alabama, she was also one of the first soccer coaches in Mobile and also coached basketball, volleyball, tennis, track and field, and softball.

When actively playing tennis, she held rankings in the Southern Lawn Tennis Association and the state of Alabama.

Bo has three adult children and six grandchildren. She lives in Mobile, "fourteen miles from the Mississippi state line" as she says where she is a writer and publisher.

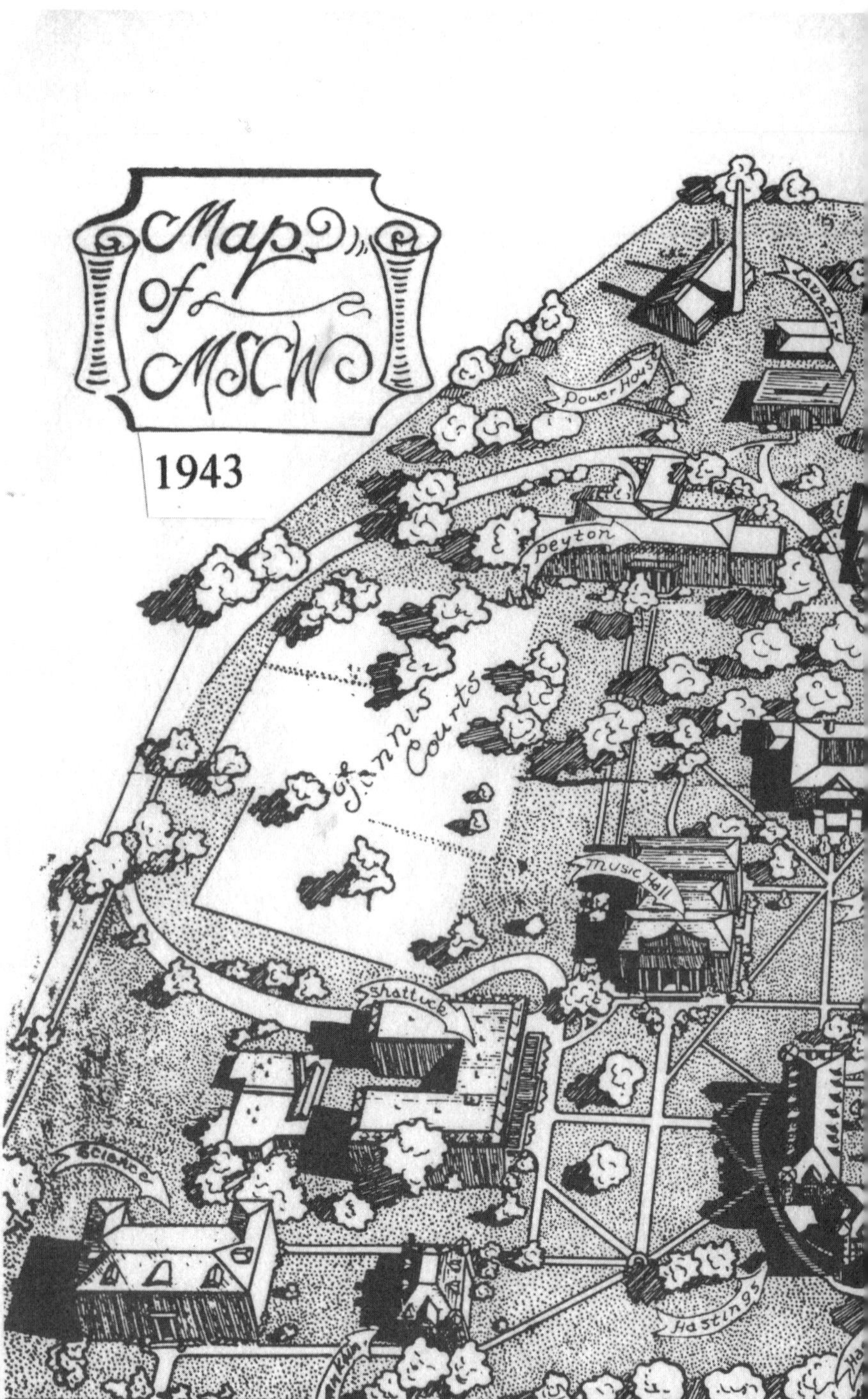
Map of MSCW
1943
Laundry
Power House
Peyton
Tennis Courts
Music Hall
Shattuck
Science
Hastings

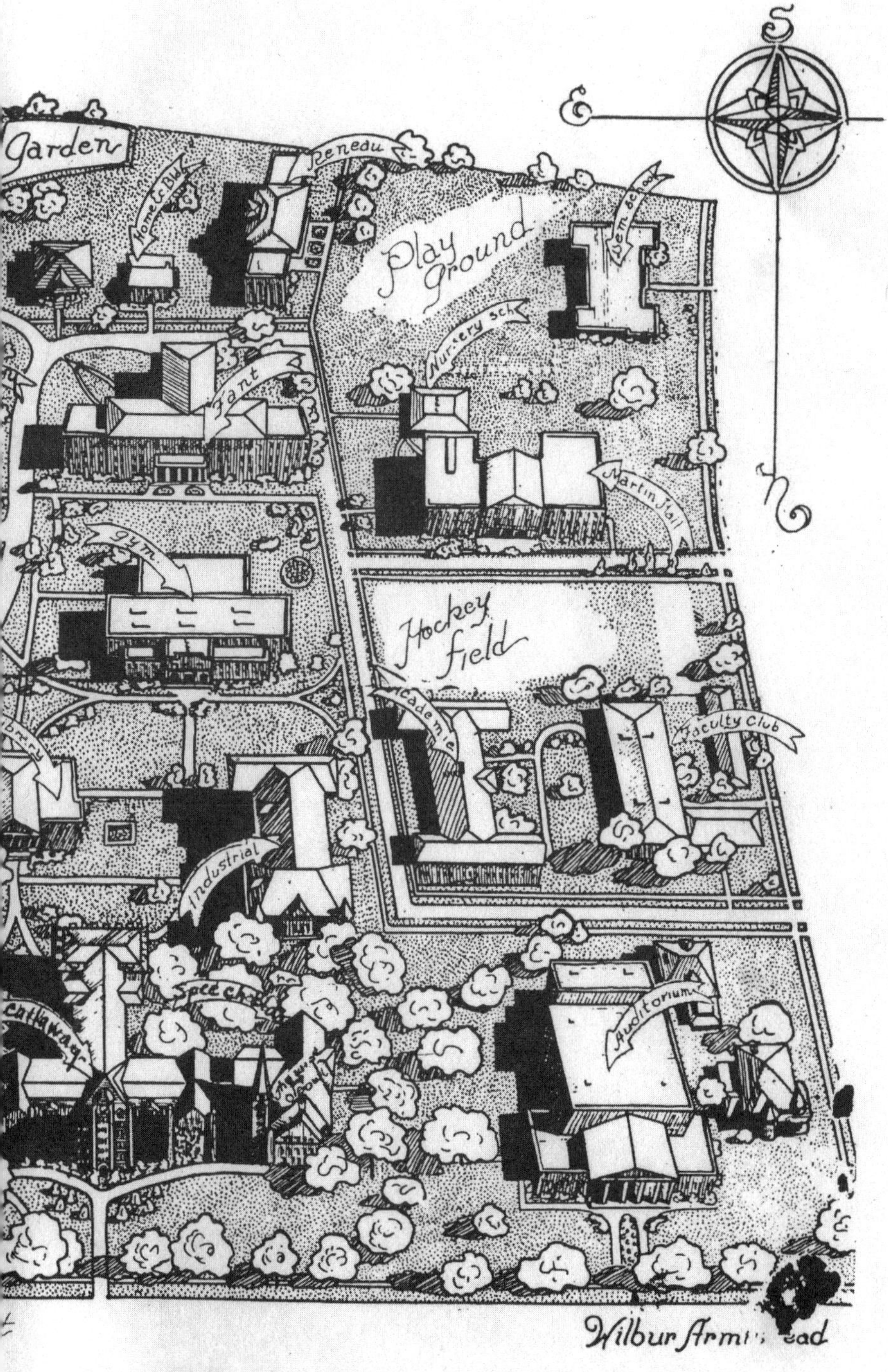
S
E
N
Garden
Home Ec Bld
Reneau
Play Ground
Dem school
Nursery sch
Fant
Martin Hall
Gym
Hockey field
Academic
Faculty Club
Industrial
Auditorium
Wilbur Arm

Mississippi University For Women
The W

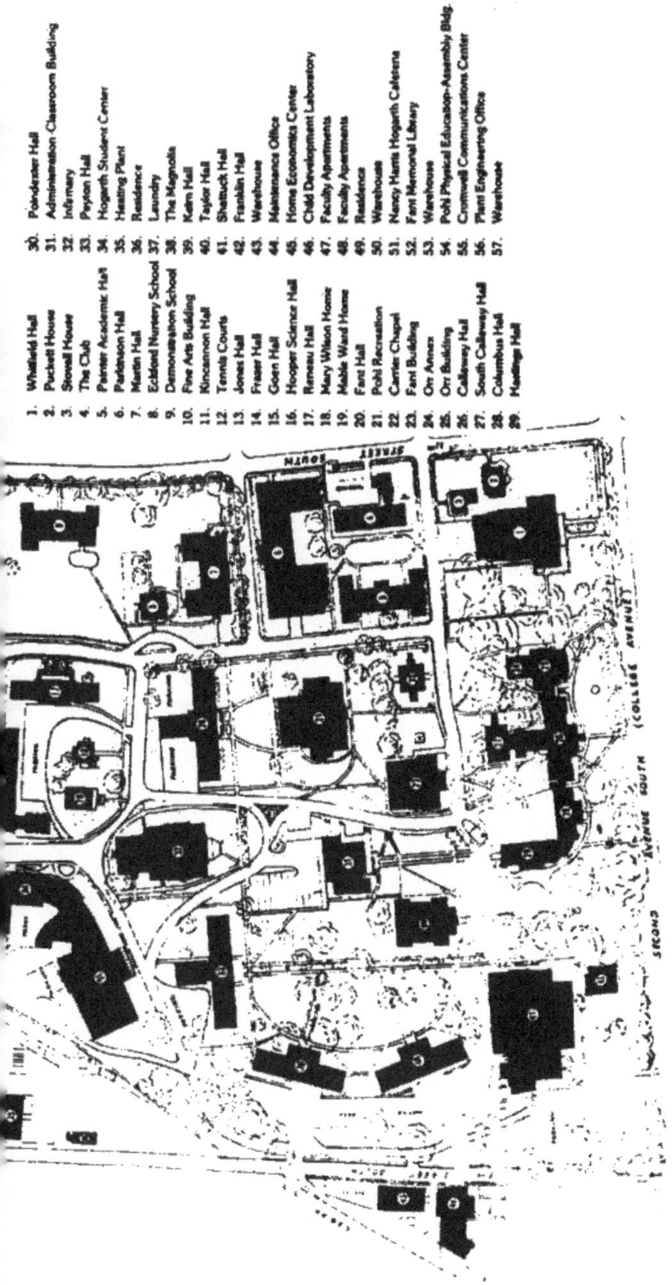
1. Whitfield Hall
2. Puckett House
3. Stovall House
4. The Club
5. Painter Academic Hall
6. Parkinson Hall
7. Martin Hall
8. Eckford Nursery School
9. Demonstration School
10. Fine Arts Building
11. Kincannon Hall
12. Tennis Courts
13. Jones Hall
14. Fraser Hall
15. Goen Hall
16. Hooper Science Hall
17. Reneau Hall
18. Mary Wilson Home
19. Mable Ward Home
20. Fant Hall
21. Pohl Recreation
22. Carrier Chapel
23. Fant Building
24. Orr Annex
25. Orr Building
26. Callaway Hall
27. South Callaway Hall
28. Columbus Hall
29. Hastings Hall
30. Poindexter Hall
31. Administration-Classroom Building
32. Infirmary
33. Peyton Hall
34. Hogarth Student Center
35. Heating Plant
36. Residence
37. Laundry
38. The Magnolia
39. Kern Hall
40. Taylor Hall
41. Shattuck Hall
42. Franklin Hall
43. Warehouse
44. Maintenance Office
45. Home Economics Center
46. Child Development Laboratory
47. Faculty Apartments
48. Faculty Apartments
49. Residence
50. Warehouse
51. Nancy Harris Hogarth Cafeteria
52. Fant Memorial Library
53. Warehouse
54. Pohl Physical Education-Assembly Bldg.
55. Cromwell Communications Center
56. Plant Engineering Office
57. Warehouse

ORDER BLANK

For extra copies of

BE GOOD SWEET MAID

Please send____copies of Be Good Sweet Maid to:

Name____

Address______________________________________

City______________________State___Zip_______

Enclose $10.95 for each copy.
POSTAGE is $2.50 for first copy, add $1.00 for
each additional copy. (Alabama residents add 4% sales tax)

Make checks payable to:

Magnolia Mansions Press,

Mail to:

Magnolia Mansions Press
4661 Pinewood Drive East
Mobile, AL 36618

FORTY-SEVEN BY TRADITION

THE SPECTATOR

GIVES TO YOU THE SOPH EDITION

Hall of Fame

MSCW Shares Grief Of A Stricken World

Methodist Youth Open New Year

Rev. Newman To Be Guest Speaker

Honor President Special Rites

Raney Presents Senior Recital

Ann Hitch Serves As Accompanist

Callaway Wins As Cleanest Dorm

Shattuck, Peyton Win High Rank

YWCA Installs 1945-46 Cabinet Members Sunday

Student Officers Attend Meeting

Fallen Leader....

Kiwanians Meet Here On Campus

ARC Worker Will Teach Three Courses Here

Debaters Place Second In Match

Four Schools Vie At ASCW Meet

Mildred Gillis Plays Recital

Officials Will Give U. S. Civil Service Examination Here

Veterans' Bureau Seeks Applicants For Appointments

Summer Lists Changes In '45-'46 Handbook

School Policy Will Emphasize Inner Discipline For Students

"Y" Announces New Committee

Retreat Is Held At Lake Norris

Latin American Authority Speaks Here Tomorrow

Mrs. McClintock Also Speaks To AAUW Members

Class Elects Davis '46 Senior President

Dean And Christian Are Chosen Junior, Soph Heads For '45-'46

Theatre Guild Will Give One Act Play

32 High School Seniors Get Conference Bids

SOPHOMORE EDITION HEADS

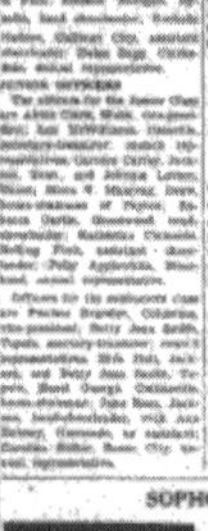

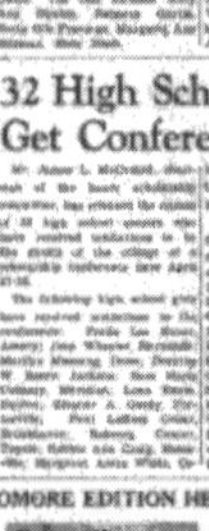